DO THE IMPOSSIBLE

HOW TO BECOME EXTRAORDINARY AND IMPACT THE WORLD AT SCALE

THIBAUT MEURISSE

CONTENTS

CONTENTS

WHO IS THIS BOOK FOR?

Many people say that they want to "change the world," but few mean it. That is, few will choose to do the actual work and pay the price. It's more comfortable for them to broadcast their noble intentions to the world than to work hard to make it happen, isn't it?

This book is intended for committed people who are willing to pay the price. It's for those who are more interested in making an impact than in being admired or famous. It's for those whose desire to help is stronger than their desire to be right and for those whose actions speak louder than their words. As Henry Ford said, "You can't build a reputation on what you are going to do."

Many people have good intentions and lofty aspirations. But, in the end, all that matters is the impact your actions actually make. The truth is, making a genuine impact is tough. *Really tough.*

And even if you were to impact millions of people's lives, in the grand scheme of things, it might not make much of a difference. So why even bother? Why try to do impossible things and become extraordinary?

To learn the answer, read on.

DOING THE IMPOSSIBLE AND BECOMING EXTRAORDINARY

When was the last time you did something that you thought would be impossible?

How did it make you feel?

Whenever you do "impossible" things, you challenge your limited sense of self. You remove the labels society has given you. You transform the story you're telling yourself. And, perhaps, more importantly, you feel alive.

Doing the impossible offers you a glimpse of your self—what it looks like, and what it's capable of becoming. The more layers of fear and self-limitation you peel away, the more you realize the immensity of the power within yourself. As a result, your "sense of self" expands, and your old self gives way to a more powerful and authentic self. In other words, as you do the impossible, you release your fear. As you destroy your limitations, you begin your path toward becoming extraordinary. Now, why should you strive to do the impossible and become extraordinary? Is it to accumulate money, gain power, or become famous?

No.

Choosing to become extraordinary is making a declaration of love to the person you see in the mirror. It's committing to giving your best, not just to contribute to the world or gather accolades, but to be able to say to yourself, "I'm proud of you."—and to actually feel it and know it to be true in your heart.

Choosing to be extraordinary is refusing to be little more than an extra in the movie of your life. Instead, you can choose to become the main character. Being extraordinary is to act in a way that makes your movie worth watching. You do this by facing your fears, moving beyond your comfort zone, and doing the seemingly impossible.

In the end, being extraordinary is a choice. It's a promise you make to yourself every day. We can all choose to be extraordinary in our unique way. As you give your best, you discover the true meaning of self-esteem. Having deeper confidence, you begin to notice changes. You act differently. You speak differently. You become more convincing. You become more real. You feel more relaxed. And, as you start to love yourself more, gaining the approval of others becomes less important.

Finally, choosing to be extraordinary is accepting your gifts and expressing them to the fullest. It's embracing your talents, skills, and personality so that you can feel good about yourself and impact the world simply by being yourself.

So, do you want to do the impossible and become extraordinary? If so, keep reading.

INTRODUCTION

Ever since I became a teenager, I've had this feeling that I would do extraordinary things. But nothing significant happened until I entered my thirties. Until that point, I felt too insecure. I wasn't smart, disciplined, or confident enough to be the next Nelson Mandela, Mahatma Gandhi, or Elon Musk. I wondered how on earth a shy, introverted guy like me could even *dream* of doing anything extraordinary.

But my biggest shock came when I joined an MBA program. All of a sudden, I had to confront the harsh reality that many people in the course were a great deal smarter than me. And it seemed that no amount of work would enable me to catch up with them. If anything, when everybody studied hard, the smartest people just kept increasing their lead over me. That was when I had to face my insecurities and my perceived "limitations".

Yet even so, the idea that I was capable of doing extraordinary things still nagged away at me. So, I had a decision to make. Would I do something about my perceived failings or would I give up and coast through life?

It took me a while, but after a great deal of soul searching, I made a discovery.

Friends had often told me that I was most passionate when talking about personal development. It gave me an idea. I thought, "There is something here. I have something within myself that I don't see in others. If I commit to my vision and work relentlessly on myself, I can inspire smart people to pursue their vision and do extraordinary things." I had what might be called an epiphany.

In that moment, I realized that I didn't have to be a genius. I realized that I could use my ability to inspire and motivate people to move toward their vision.

So, I began to write. And I didn't stop. Over time, book sales increased. One day, a Japanese publisher offered to distribute my book. Another day a Chinese publisher contacted me, and so it continued. Eventually, my books were being published in more than twenty languages.

The truth is, while trying to inspire others, I was also trying to inspire myself. Writing acted as a therapy. And it helped me discover that I was more capable than I could ever have imagined. So, I started wondering what my limits were. What could I achieve if I give it my all? Who could I become? What was the greatest possible impact I could have on the world?

But, for a while, I got lost.

I relied on my past accomplishments and stopped giving my best.

While other people were impressed by my results, I wasn't. I had forgotten the lessons I teach others: we are successful in life when we do the best we can *today*. Success is a process—and it never ends. Success is who we are, and we must embody it every day. So, I went back to the drawing board. I told myself that I had done nothing, that I knew nothing and that the best was yet to come. I let go of my past accomplishments and behaved as though I were penniless, unsuccessful and that I had to prove myself all over again. Most importantly, I realized that there was only one person I needed to impress: the man in the mirror.

I wanted to be able to say to myself, "I'm proud of you, Thibaut," and to feel it deep inside my heart.

So, I came to a decision. I would become extraordinary.

In the process, I learned a key lesson. Most people are selling themselves way too short. They inhabit a tiny version of themselves, one who is filled with negative assumptions and self-imposed limitations. The writer, Steven Pressfield, wrote that, "*Most of us have two lives. The life we live, and the unlived life within us.*" And, unfortunately, the unlived life within us is usually far larger than the life we actually do live.

The premise of this book is simple. There are people who can impact the world at scale and help millions. This book is here to serve as a guide. It's here to wake up the talented people who have lived way too small for way too long. It's here to give them permission to share more of themselves instead of hiding behind fears, self-imposed limitations and excuses.

If you can relate to this intention, read this book. Then, use it to move from ordinary to extraordinary. Let go of layers of limitations and start uncovering what you're capable of becoming. Keep impressing yourself by doing impossible things. Get a taste for what it means to expand beyond your limited sense of self.

Throughout this book, we'll go over what you need to know to utilize your talent and skills to help you become extraordinary and impact the world at scale.

In **Part I. Fundamental Assumptions and Models of Reality**, I will challenge you to update your beliefs and think bigger than you've ever thought before. We'll discuss what assumptions are and how they shape your life. We'll discuss the eight principles that drive most human behavior. You'll also learn the three laws of belief and three key beliefs (Meta-Beliefs) that will profoundly impact everything you do.

In **Part II. Applying Extreme Leverage**, we will delve into the eight different sources of leverage that you must use to increase the power of your actions exponentially. This includes the size and quality of your thoughts, your thinking skills, your personal growth, technology, your focus, other people's time, money, and knowledge.

By reading this book, you will acquire the framework that you need to scale your impact and make a difference. You'll discover why making a big impact is all about accumulating energy and channeling it effectively. And you'll also learn how to do so intentionally.

In truth, you have far more power than you can imagine. You would need many lifetimes to reach the limits of your capacity. Unfortunately, you only have one lifetime. Let's ensure you make the most of your lifetime by using as much of your potential as possible.

So, are you ready to embark on a journey of exponential growth, extreme scale, and massive impact? If so, read on.

YOUR FREE STEP-BY-STEP WORKBOOK

To help you become extraordinary, I've created a workbook as a companion guide to this book. Make sure you download it at the following URL:

https://whatispersonaldevelopment.org/do-the-impossible

If you have any difficulties downloading the workbook, contact me at:

thibaut.meurisse@gmail.com and I'll send it to you as soon as possible.

Alternatively, you can also use the workbook available at the end of this book.

PART I

FUNDAMENTAL ASSUMPTIONS AND MODELS OF REALITY

Are you good at analyzing people? Would you say you have a solid understanding of how reality works?

To impact the world at scale, you must operate under the correct assumptions. That is, you must refine your thinking and understand human psychology and the nature of reality at the deepest level possible. This is because the quality of your thinking determines the impact your actions have on the world.

In this section, we'll see how your assumptions rule your life. We'll discuss how to replace ineffective assumptions with effective ones. In addition, we'll explore what models of reality are, and we'll give you all the tools you need to build a powerful model.

1

FUNDAMENTAL ASSUMPTIONS ABOUT HUMAN BEINGS

When seeking to improve the world, many well-intentioned people commit the critical mistake of wanting to change other people. As a result, they design systems, create philosophies, or implement political ideas that go against human nature.

This never works.

These people may feel good about themselves for developing wonderful ideas, but these ideas are a waste of time at best and harmful at worst. It's not unlike people who marry someone hoping that they will be able to change their spouse.

This rarely works.

Understanding human psychology is one of the key aspects required for any person who wants to become more impactful. If cult leaders can amass millions of followers, there's a reason for it. They must know something you don't. To impact the world at scale, you must understand the key principles that guide most human behavior. In this section, we're going to explore the following eight principles:

1. Energy is the currency of the world.
2. We have far more potential than we can ever imagine.

3. Incentives rule the world.
4. Fear and love are the two fundamental forces that drive human behavior.
5. Most of us want to be part of something bigger than ourselves.
6. Most of us don't know what we want (and will follow people who *do* know what they want).
7. We all believe we're right.
8. We're always trying to convince others of something.

Let's review each of these principles in detail and see why they matter.

1) Energy is the currency of the world

Our world is made of energy. Understanding how it works and how to channel it effectively is key to achieving any ambitious goal.

The first thing to understand is that energy can only produce results in the real world when it's channeled effectively. Therefore, anyone who aspires to impact the world at scale must channel energy in one way or another. When scattered, energy is weakened and has little effect on anything. Imagine if every employee in a company worked toward a different goal. What would happen? The company wouldn't be able to deliver quality products or services. For this reason, companies need to establish a clear vision and create a culture. This enables employees to know how they should behave and what they should be doing (i.e., where to channel their energy).

The same principle applies to individuals. Someone who scatters their focus and tackles too many projects at the same time will struggle to do anything significant in their life. By creating a clear vision and striving toward a specific goal, a person can channel their energy and make a decisive impact on the world.

You *cannot* skip this step. You must become a master at channeling both your energy and the energy of people around you. You must draw people, resources, and attention toward you and your vision. This is the *only* way to impact the world at scale. If you want to make an impact on the world, the key question you must ask yourself is this:

"What can I do to channel as much energy as possible toward the realization of my vision?"

Now, let's see how energy circulates so that you can channel more of it.

A. Thoughts (potential energy)

Your thoughts are the most powerful tool you have to transform yourself and the world around you. They're the only thing you ever have (some) control over. To increase your influence, you must increase the quality of your thoughts. You must refine your thoughts and treat them with the utmost respect. You must guard your mind against the disempowering thoughts of the people around you.

However, thoughts are only *potential* energy. Just having the idea that you want to achieve extraordinary things or "change the world" means nothing in and of itself. Thoughts only gain power when given the gift of your attention. It's your repeated attention that energizes your thoughts.

B. Attention (focused energy)

Attention enables you to channel the *potential* energy of thoughts. When you give *attention* to your thoughts over and over, they'll begin to permeate everything you do.

In fact, attention is the new oil in today's economy. Everyone is fighting for your attention, and there are good reasons for this. Companies know that the more they can grab your attention, the more money they can make. This is why they invest so much money in marketing. For instance, household names like Coca-Cola spend billions every year to market their products. Why? Because they want to penetrate your mind. They want to permeate the culture and become a part of the collective consciousness. Similarly, social media companies and video streaming services try to keep you hooked for the same reason.

In short, companies hijack your attention to make money. Remember, your attention is one of the most powerful tools you have. Your ability to give your attention to what matters enables you to create the life you desire. By channeling your attention toward what you want, you can impact the world. When you lose this ability, you lose your power.

What do you think I'm trying to do with this book?

Yes, I'm trying to hook you. And I've been quite successful so far (otherwise you wouldn't still be reading). Why would I do that? To make money? Sure. But also because the only way I can hope to impact your life positively is by capturing your attention. Once you're listening, I can nudge you to do either something you want to do, or something I'd like you to do. The point is, to impact millions of people, you must both:

1. Energize your thoughts by giving them your attention consistently over a long period of time, and

2. Learn to grab the attention of people you want to impact.

C. Money (stored energy)

Few people understand what money is and how it works. Quite simply, money is stored time and energy. For instance:

- Your salary represents the amount of time and effort you've spent at work.
- Your savings are the accumulation of the time and energy you dedicated to working—that you didn't spend on rent, food, leisure activities, et cetera.
- Your debts are the amount of time and energy you owe to someone.

Money is a time and energy saving mechanism. Without money, we wouldn't be able to store our energy (the fruits of our labor). Retirement would be impossible, and we would be forced to work forever. Money matters because it is time/energy saved. Furthermore, the more time and energy you possess, the more impact you can have on the world.

D. Organizations (organized energy)

There is only so much we can do by ourselves, which is why we tend to collaborate and create organizations. The purpose of an organization is to accumulate the energy of its members and to use it to achieve specific goals (delivering products, funding projects, solving issues, et cetera).

To impact the world at scale, you need help. You cannot generate enough energy to impact the lives of millions of people by yourself. There are many ways to accumulate energy. It can be by building teams, by outsourcing tasks, by using technologies such as the internet or by using a combination of all three.

To conclude, energy is the currency of this world. Your ability to accumulate it over time and channel it effectively toward the realization of your vision is key. The more energy you accumulate, the more potential power you have. If you learn only one thing from this book, remember this:

You must use all the forms of leverage available to channel as much energy as you can toward your vision.

2) We have far more potential than we can ever imagine

Another fundamental truth about human beings is that we have infinitely more potential than we imagine. However, to utilize this potential, we face an irreconcilable dilemma:

Our potential is almost unlimited, but our time is highly restricted.

For this reason, the key question to keep in the back of your mind is:

"What is the best way to spend my time, energy, and resources during the limited time I am given on this planet?"

You can always acquire new skills. If you are determined enough, you can become great at almost anything you put effort into. This is true of everyone you encounter. Therefore, to impact the world, you need to understand the following:

1. You have barely scratched the surface of what is possible for you, and

2. Countless people around you have untapped potential waiting to be activated (by you).

3) Incentives rule the world

Incentives are the oil that lubricates the world and makes it run effectively. People are most likely to act when they have a good reason to do so. Remove the incentives and, soon enough, they'll stop giving their best.

Making a significant impact on the world requires that you understand psychology, evolutionary biology, and a whole lot of other disciplines. It demands that you see the world as it *is*, not as you *wish* it would be. If you give the right incentives to people around you, they will act in ways that support your vision. But if you fail to do so, things are likely to go wrong at some point.

As the famous investor, Charlie Munger, once said, *"Show me the incentives, I'll show you the outcome."*

This is why you must be deliberate in the way you provide incentives to people working with you. Whenever you give a specific target to employees, freelancers, or contractors, their focus will be on hitting that target. If you set a good target, one that is aligned with your goal or vision, incentives will be effective. However, if you set the wrong target, people will often act in counterproductive ways, and this will lead to unintended consequences.

Put simply, people tend to do what they're evaluated on and rewarded for. Therefore, your job is to identify the key activities and performance indicators that are most likely to produce the results you want. Then, you must assess and reward the people who work with or under you accordingly.

4) Fear and Love are the two fundamental forces driving human behavior

At any time, you're acting either out of fear or out of love. Your intention should be to act more out of love than out of fear.

When you act out of fear, you try to "get" something from people, whether it's their attention, their money or their approval. This idea of "getting" is related to the concept of ego. In other words, you attempt to feel better by attaching yourself to something external. If you can make people like you, then your ego will be satisfied. Or if you can find the right person to love, you will be complete. In short, you live under the false idea that you can add something to the essence of who you are. Furthermore, if you add enough "stuff," you'll reach a point where you finally feel good enough.

This doesn't work.

This is like adding layers of clothes and putting on make-up, hoping that it will change you at your core. In truth, you cannot add anything to who you already are, you can only let go of artificial limitations, illusory fears, and poor conditioning to reveal your true character and your inner potential. Now, you can certainly enjoy people's company, things, or other people's attention, but you can't *possess* anything. You can own things in the legal sense, but nothing and nobody can ever *belong to you*.

Conversely, when you act out of love, your focus is on giving. You give your time, your attention, your money, or your unique gifts to the people around you. You express yourself and attempt to show your true personality rather than creating a persona to match the individual you *think* you should be. When you act out of love, you practice letting go of your desire to take, and focus instead on giving unconditionally.

Here is another way to see it.

When you act out of fear, you see the world as a zero-sum game. There isn't enough for everybody. So, you must take as much as possible while you still can. On the other hand, when you act out of love, you see the world as a pie that can grow. You understand that, by contributing in your unique way, you can help people tap into their potential. And by sharing more of yourself, you can increase the pie.

What you believe determines what you do and how you impact the world. If you focus on taking from others, you'll perceive the world as a dog-eat-dog place, reinforcing that collective narrative. However, if you focus on giving to the world, you feed and grow the narrative that we can all have more if we all give more.

So, how often are you acting out of fear? That is, how often are you trying to get things from others for your selfish needs? And how often are you acting out of love? That is, how much do you express yourself and give to others whether it be your time, your money, or your attention?

Remember, at any time, you are acting either out of love or out of fear. Whenever you can, try to act a little more out of love.

5) Most people don't know what they want (and will follow those who do know what they want)

Many people don't know what they want. They never think of how they'd like their life to be. They lack an exciting vision to propel them forward. As a result, they wander through life, hoping for the best.

As Mark Twain said, "*I can teach anybody how to get what they want out of life. The problem is that I can't find anybody who can tell me what they want.*" Knowing what you want out of life is hard. Clarity isn't something that happens spontaneously. It requires both the courage to look within yourself and the willingness to act and reflect on a regular basis. In other words, gaining clarity is a process that requires commitment.

Clarity also demands that you take action. By acting, you gather information about what you enjoy and don't enjoy. You create new opportunities and learn more about yourself—your values, your interests, and your skills—but also about the issues you need to work on. Most people lack clarity. By developing enough clarity and establishing a specific vision, you can convince people way smarter than you to become part of that vision. See clarity as a skill to be practiced. Ask yourself what you want and take more action to obtain it.

What about you? Do you have a clear vision of where you want to be in five or ten years from now? If not, that's okay. Start building your vision today and keep refining it over time.

6) Most people want to be part of something bigger than themselves

Most people aspire to fight for a noble cause that will improve the world, but they are often scared of pursuing an ambitious vision on their own. Therefore, if your vision is exciting enough, it will inspire others to follow you. But for this to happen, you must be willing to ask for help and allow others to become part of your vision.

The bottom line is this. Show the world what your vision will look like. Infuse your unstoppable enthusiasm into people around you. Then, see who's in.

7) We all believe we're right

We all believe our way of seeing the world is the correct one. If we didn't, we would change our beliefs immediately. For instance, people tend to believe that their political beliefs, religious beliefs, and perception of the world is right.

This means that you're probably wrong on many topics. For this reason, you must stay humble and keep upgrading your model of reality. The more you see reality as it actually is, the more power you will have to affect it. The more you align yourself with the truth, the more you can act in a way that creates tangible results. As the entrepreneur, Elon Musk, says, your goal should be to *be less wrong.* As most people think they're right, don't expect them to buy into your vision or to agree with everything you say.

Accept the fact that we're all "right." And, rather than trying to convince others, listen to them. Try to understand their point of view better. Active listening and sincere curiosity are the first steps toward influencing people.

People must feel as though they're being heard before they can even consider changing their minds.

Everyone is right—or so they think. Remember this principle as you're moving toward your extraordinary vision.

8) We're always trying to convince others

Whether we know it or not, we're in the selling business. Throughout the day, we try to convince others to act in a way beneficial to us and/or to them. For instance:

- Parents try to encourage their children to eat more vegetables,
- Spouses try to sell each other on what house they should buy, or how they should educate their kids,
- Single people try to convince their date that they are a good prospect,
- CEOs try to make their employees buy into their vision, and
- Marketers try to convince people to buy the products or services they are promoting.

The point is this. You are a salesperson. You must sell everyone around you on your vision. It requires that you gain clarity and build unshakeable belief. If you don't sell others on your vision, they will sell you on theirs—and you'll work on making *their* vision come true rather than fulfilling *your* vision. There's nothing wrong with that, *per se*, but if you're reading this book that is probably not what you signed up for.

Once you grasp these eight principles about the human condition, your actions will have far more impact on the world around you.

Now, let's explore what assumptions are, how they shape your reality and what you can do to make them work for you.

* * *

Action steps

Using your action guide:

- Assess how extraordinary you currently are in various areas of your life.
- Produce your own list of "impossible" things to strive for.

2

THE POWER OF ASSUMPTIONS

In life, there are three things you seem to have control over. These are:

- Your thoughts,
- Your words, and
- Your actions.

How well you control your thoughts, words, and actions will determine the results you'll obtain. But the words that you use when talking to yourself or to others result from your thoughts. This means that there are actually only two things you control:

- Your thoughts, and
- Your actions.

Now, your actions don't occur out of nowhere. Before you can act, a signal must be sent to your brain. In other words, your actions are also based on the thoughts that you're having. Therefore, to simplify further, there is only one thing you can control (partially):

- Your thoughts.

And your thoughts don't appear out of nowhere either. They're the result of your beliefs. These beliefs come from the assumptions that you make about yourself and the world. This is why, to change your life, you must change the one and only thing that determines the actions that you take (or fail to take):

- Your assumptions.

To summarize, it works like this:

Assumptions —> beliefs system —> thoughts —> words —> actions —> results.

What's an assumption?

In this book, I define an assumption as "a statement that you believe to be true." That statement dictates (and usually constrains) what you allow yourself to think. Some examples are:

- I'm not the type of person who...
- I'm not very smart.
- I could never do X, Y, or Z.

Now, consider the following assumption:

I can do anything I set my mind to.

This simple statement expands your field of possibility and unlocks your potential. By believing it, you remove many of the assumptions that are holding you back. Now, below are some examples of how you could reframe the assumptions mentioned above:

- I'm not the type of person who achieves things, *but* if I have a compelling enough reason and I am willing to put in the time and effort required, there is almost nothing I cannot do.
- I might not be as smart as I'd like to be yet, *but* I can learn the skills and gather the resources that I need to reach my goals.

- I can't do X, Y, or Z now, *but* with enough training, proper mentoring, and strong motivation, I can become that type of person.

What about you? What assumptions are you living by, and how are they limiting your extraordinary potential?

Most people assume that they can't do something before they even try. To transform your life, invert your thinking. Assume everything is possible until you have proven with relentless action that it isn't. As you do so, you'll discover that you have dramatically underestimated what you are capable of achieving.

* * *

Action steps

Complete the following exercise in your action guide:

- In what ways are you currently limiting yourself?
- Identify three disempowering assumptions that are preventing you from achieving your goals.
- Alternatively, think of one major goal you'd like to achieve but don't believe is possible for you. Then, write down all the reasons or excuses for why you believe it can't be done.

3

THE THREE LAWS OF BELIEF

The world obeys specific laws. When you fail to learn the rules, you've lost the game before it has even begun.

Our ability to believe is one of the most powerful tools we have. Unlike any other living creature, we can use imagination to envision our ideal future and make it a reality. We are the only species on earth given such a gift. Therefore, make sure to use your extraordinary ability to believe and achieve anything that you want in life. Below are three laws that will help you make the most of the power of belief.

#1—Law of choice

The first law of belief is that you can choose to believe anything you desire. You can believe that the earth is flat, that Santa Claus exists, or that lizards rule the world. And you can update any belief at will. At any time, you can decide to replace disempowering or inaccurate beliefs with more empowering and useful ones. This is a necessary step if you want to transform your life and impact the world around you. If you keep struggling, it's probably because you hold onto disempowering beliefs. If so, ask yourself the following question:

What is preventing me from achieving my goals?

Perhaps, you don't believe it's possible. If that's the case, take the first step—as small as it may be—and strengthen your beliefs using the exercises in this book. Over time, and as you take more action, you will reinforce your beliefs and begin to eliminate self-doubt.

Remember, what you believe always comes with consequences, which leads to the second law.

#2—Law of cause and effect

The second law of belief is that what you believe affects your life. Your thoughts dictate your actions and come with real consequences in the world. Consequently, as you change your beliefs, you will change your life.

For example, if you believe you can't do something, whether it's writing a book, running a marathon, or speaking on stage, you will never give yourself a chance to succeed in these challenges. However, in truth, you can *always* do more than you believe is possible.

#3—Law of repetition

The third law of belief states that you can dramatically increase the intensity and power of your thoughts through repetition. Thoughts are potential waiting to be activated. By repeating a thought in your head, you make it part of your model of reality. This, in turn, affects how you feel and what you do, and will inevitably impact your environment. To make a greater impact, intensify your beliefs and build unshakeable conviction in your ability to succeed.

For example, having the thought you'd like to run a marathon or lose weight isn't enough. You must turn your thought into an action, an obsession until it becomes ingrained in your mind. When you believe running a marathon or reaching your ideal weight is inevitable—and act accordingly—you will bring about astonishing changes.

Let's look at a concrete example that illustrates these three laws.

Imagine that you dislike your job and want to do something more meaningful, but don't think it's possible. Feeling hopeless, you stay in the same job for years or, perhaps even, for the rest of your life.

Now, using the *law of choice*, you can choose to believe whatever you desire. You've noticed people doing more meaningful work. So, you choose to believe that you can do the same. You adopt the belief, "I can do meaningful work, work I enjoy, and I can make money from it."

Equipped with this new belief, you begin to act differently (*law of cause an effect*). You ask yourself what you really want to do. You reflect on past projects. You chat to friends about your strengths and weaknesses, you upgrade your skills, and you look for more suitable jobs.

Then, using the *law of repetition*, you repeatedly focus on the thought that "you can and will design a career you enjoy." You envision yourself being fulfilled at work. You gather case studies of people with meaningful careers. As you do so, you strengthen the belief that you can make money doing something you enjoy. Then, as you keep moving toward your goal, it turns into a reality.

Think of it this way. For almost anything you believe impossible, someone else is doing it or has done it before. So, why can't you do it too? The human mind has the extraordinary ability to turn almost any dream into reality. But this starts by choosing what you want to believe, visualizing yourself as having reached your desired goal, and acting accordingly.

These three laws of belief become even more powerful once you make specific beliefs—Meta-Beliefs—part of your belief system.

* * *

Action steps

Complete the corresponding exercises in your action guide.

4

THE THREE META-BELIEFS THAT RULE ALL BELIEFS

Extraordinary results require extraordinary beliefs. To do the extraordinary, you must leverage the power of beliefs more effectively than anybody else. This starts by adopting rock-solid Meta-Beliefs you can use to impact the world.

What are Meta-Beliefs?

Your beliefs don't all have the same value. While one small belief may have insignificant impact, one major belief can revolutionize your life. In short, there is a hierarchy. Meta-Beliefs are the beliefs at the top of the tree. They make all the other beliefs possible. They act like a valve. When that valve is opened, the field of possibility flows freely, enabling you to express your full potential. However, when the valve is obstructed, that field becomes restricted. Once internalized deeply, the following three Meta-Beliefs will restructure your belief system and change everything:

1. Everything is possible,
2. Everything is learnable, and
3. Every problem is solvable.

Let's look at each of these Meta-Beliefs in detail.

Meta Belief #1—Everything is possible.

Many people wait for permission to do what they want. They need a sign from the universe that they are good enough. They need their friends to give them their approval, or they need their parents to believe in them.

People on their path toward extraordinary results think differently. They believe they can achieve anything they set their minds to. What their friends think is possible (or impossible) for them is irrelevant. They understand that everything starts from within. Therefore, they practice believing in themselves instead of waiting for other people's approval or support.

When I decided I wanted to inspire millions of people through my writing, nobody cheered me on. With no audience, no network, and no serious writing experience, publishing books in a competitive market and in a foreign language didn't seem like the best idea. The odds were against me. But I chose to believe it was possible, I visualized the reality I wanted to create, and I kept working on my goals for years. Was it hard? Yes. Incredibly hard. But extraordinary results require an extraordinary level of self-belief.

The good news is that you don't need to wait for others to believe in you. You only need to believe in yourself. And you can start doing so today.

Remember, in life you have two choices:

- You can assume that you can't do things you've not done before and stay where you are, or
- You can assume that you can do anything you set your mind to and progress toward the person you wish to become.

Average people stay in the comfort of what they already know. They pile up excuses to justify why they can't achieve their goals. As a result, their self-imposed limitations become their reality. On the other hand, outstanding people believe that everything is possible. They understand that, many times through history, people have done things considered impossible. So, to be on the safe side, they assume that *everything* is possible. Then, they decide to move toward their impossible goals.

As Mark Twain once said, *"They did not know it was impossible, so they did it."* Once upon a time, it was thought that running a mile in less than four minutes was impossible. But, one day, Roger Bannister broke the four-minute barrier. Today, over one thousand people have done it too. Similarly:

- Retired Navy SEAL, David Goggins, ran an ultramarathon with barely any preparation.
- Entrepreneur, Elon Musk, created a rocket company from scratch and succeeded against all odds.
- Sixty-one-year-old farmer, Cliff Young, ran for five days straight without sleeping and won a 544-mile race, wearing overalls and work boots.
- Wim Hof ran a full marathon through the Namibian desert without drinking any water.

The point is, each of us has a far greater potential than we imagine. We can inhabit the comfort of our own bubble, or we can break through our limits and do the impossible.

Why not make "everything is possible" your default assumption? Why not take the first step toward achieving your impossible goals?

Now, let's look at a few specific beliefs that will help you ingrain this Meta-Belief in your mind.

Sub-belief #1—If someone else has done it before, so can I

Many of your goals have been achieved before by people no smarter than you. One belief that had a profound impact on my life is the idea that, "If someone else can, I can too."

You can easily convince yourself that others have had an easier time of it than you, that they are more gifted, or were brought up in a more favorable environment. Yes, some of these things may be true, but you can also overestimate the differences between your brain and everyone else's brain. Generally speaking, you were born with more or less the same brain capacity as other people. And your brain is malleable. In most cases, what someone else has learned to do, with enough time and effort, you can learn to do as well. In the end, it boils down to one simple thing:

the strength of your "whys."

If you want something badly enough, you will usually find a way. If not, you'll find an excuse. Remember, if someone else can do it, you can probably do it too. This belief helped me go from being an unknown author to becoming a successful one. Use it to achieve outstanding results in your life.

Sub-belief #2—If one, then one million

You don't need to worry about how you're going to reach your ultimate vision, but you do need to take the first step. According to this sub-belief, if you can do something just one time, then you can do it over and over and repeat the success. Here are some examples:

- If you can find one client to coach, you can find five, ten, twenty or one hundred clients.
- If you can make one dollar online, you can make $10, $100, $10, 000 or $1,000,000 dollars online.
- If you can just lose one kilo of bodyweight, you can lose five, ten, twenty, or thirty kilos.
- If you can train yourself to run one mile, you can build up to run two, five, or ten miles.

The bottom line is this. You only need to do something challenging once. Yes, it will be hard, but if you can do it once, you can repeat the process and be successful again. Therefore, do whatever you can to reach that first milestone. Run your first mile. Lose your first kilo. Find your first client. Make your first sale. Write your first paragraph. Then, *know* and *believe* that you can repeat the process until you achieve your goals.

If you can do something once, you can do it again. And again. And again. This is inevitable.

Sub-belief #3—Just because it hasn't been done before doesn't mean it cannot be done at all

We tend to believe everything has already been invented or achieved. As a result, we struggle to envision a future that is radically different from our present reality. However, one thing is certain. Many things that have never been done before will be done in the coming years. One hundred years ago, nobody could have predicted the internet. And once the internet had arrived, no one could have guessed we would be using websites and applications like YouTube, Twitter, TikTok, or Instagram. The point is that things that are commonplace now would have seemed like science fiction in the past. And what will be commonplace in twenty years isn't available right now.

Consequently, don't limit yourself by believing something cannot be done. Stop projecting the past into the future. We don't change the world by acting the same way today as we did yesterday. Instead, allow yourself to do things that have never been done before. Not everything has been invented or developed yet. We can improve things. Given time and the right amount of application, we can solve many of the issues we currently face.

To sum up. Cultivate the belief that *everything is possible*. Realize that you don't know what you're capable of achieving. It's only by seeking to go beyond what's possible that you will achieve the "impossible". And the only way to discover your limits is to progress toward your impossible goals and prove to yourself that they are indeed impossible. As you do so, you'll discover your potential is far greater than you imagined.

Assume everything is possible. Then, act today to achieve your "impossible" goals.

Remember:

- If someone else can, you can too,
- If you can do something just once, you can do it again, and

- Just because it hasn't been done before, it doesn't mean it cannot be done at all.

Meta-Belief #2—Everything is learnable

Your ability to learn is almost limitless. Whatever you believe you can do, is possible to accomplish if:

1. You believe you can do it, and
2. You keep practicing over and over.

Many people fail to realize that they can learn almost anything they want in any area of their lives. These individuals believe they can learn certain things but not others. However, in life, everything is learnable. Once you understand that everything can be learned with enough time, effort, and with the right mindset, you will begin to overcome your limitations. For instance, you will be able to acquire the following "skills":

Personal development

- How to focus better
- How to feel more grateful
- How to forgive
- How to develop more clarity

Business

- How to sell a product or service
- How to manage a team
- How to delegate
- How to speak with more confidence

Relationships

- How to communicate your needs clearly
- How to build intimacy
- How to listen actively

- How to set healthy boundaries

Skills

- How to drive a car
- How to cook
- How to speak in public
- How to write clearly

These are just a few examples. Once you truly understand that you can learn anything you decide to, your life will change dramatically. Every time you require a new skill, you'll simply practice that skill over and over. In the end, it's all about repeating something often enough until it becomes part of who you are.

Now, let's look at specific beliefs that you can adopt to make the Meta-Belief that everything is learnable more tangible and easier to apply in the real world.

Sub-belief #1—I can always improve

Adopting the belief that everything is learnable entails believing that you can and will become better at anything you put time and effort into. This belief is critical to anyone who aspires to transform their life. Because, if you don't believe you can improve and that your effort will be rewarded, why bother trying to learn anything new in the first place?

Fortunately, the idea that you can improve isn't just a belief. It's a fact. Humans are *designed* to learn and improve. You just have to take the necessary actions, learn from setbacks, and keep going. When toddlers try to walk they don't give up because "it's too hard." Despite multiple "failures," they keep trying for as long as necessary until they manage to walk. Giving up is not an option.

For any skill you desire to acquire, adopt the same mindset. Be like a toddler. Decide that you will *not* quit until you learn it. Understand that improving is an inevitability. Keep practicing. Ask for feedback. Analyze your "failures". Then, keep trying. With the proper mindset, you'll be amazed at all the things you can learn. And remember that everything is a skill. This includes technical skills, such as coding, repairing engines, or sewing clothes, but it also includes "soft" skills such as building discipline, cultivating courage, or being more empathetic.

The bottom line is this. The missing key to achieving extraordinary things is the unshakeable belief that you *can become better at anything you desire*. Make this belief yours. Then, act accordingly.

Sub-belief #2—I'm not good enough yet, but I inevitably will be

Let me guess. You feel inadequate. You doubt your ability. You don't feel good enough. We all experience feelings of inadequacy. This is part of being human.

Now, let's be honest. In certain areas of your life, you're *not* good enough (yet). That is, you're not where you want to be *yet*. You know you're capable of more—and you are right. But this is a good thing. The first step toward achieving extraordinary results is to face this harsh truth:

I am not good enough. I am going to have to improve. And this is going to suck for a while.

Whenever you feel inadequate or say to yourself that you aren't good enough, I want you to say the following instead:

I'm not as good as I'd like to be *yet*, but with work, I inevitably will be.

The word "yet" is key because it implies that you will eventually improve and succeed. For instance, you can say to yourself things like:

- I'm not as good of a speaker as I'd like to be *yet*, but I'm getting there.
- I'm not as good of a partner as I'd like to be *yet*, but I'm making progress.
- I'm not as good of a leader as I'd like to be *yet*, but I'm improving.

You're right. You're probably not good enough yet, but with practice and over time, you *will* inevitably become better.

Sub-belief #3— I am an unstoppable learner

While we can learn almost anything we desire, we often fail to do so for various reasons. Ego often holds us back. Being afraid of looking stupid, we don't ask for help. Feeling ashamed of not knowing how to do something (yet), we hide and pretend we already have the skills.

This has been a problem for me in the past. I would often assume I should know how to do something even though I'd never done it before. For instance, I hadn't used spreadsheets much before joining business school. But most of my classmates had been using them for years. During projects, I would rely on other team members for any spreadsheet-related tasks. Ashamed of myself, I was trying to hide the fact that I could barely use the software.

Believing "everything is learnable" means being willing to face discomfort in order to learn everything you need to reach your goals. It entails accepting being the dumbest person in the room. Learning something new will feel uncomfortable at first. You might experience a sense of inferiority. You might doubt yourself. You might want to hide or give up. But you *must* go past that initial feeling.

Start prioritizing learning over ego. To do so, adopt the identity of a student. Judge yourself based on how fast and how well you can learn —not based on how "right" you seem to be. Surround yourself with people who are better than you and learn to derive a sense of pleasure from learning as much as you can. Understand this: you can focus on being right, or you can learn. You can protect your ego and remain mediocre, or you can obsess over learning and become extraordinary.

Extraordinary people are extraordinary learners. They are willing to do whatever it takes to acquire the skills that they need to reach their goals. Be like them. Be extraordinary.

You *are* an unstoppable learner. Become obsessed with learning. Make it your absolute priority. Do this, and you will soon realize that you can learn anything you want in life.

Sub-belief #4—I ask for help whenever I need to

You only exist and are where you are today because of the work of other people. Each product or service you buy, or use, requires the coordination of countless people. All the technologies you enjoy today are the results of centuries of innovation.

You are *not* self-made. Nobody is.

I'm pointing this out because many of us want to do everything on our own. We are arrogant enough to believe we don't need anyone's help to reach our goals. However, this couldn't be further from the truth. Consequently, be willing to ask for help. Swallow your pride and ego and learn from others. Ask for advice. Hire people. Read books. Don't try to reinvent the wheel.

Extraordinary people are always looking for ways to learn and increase their impact. Ordinary people tend to believe that they should do everything on their own, but without the help of others, they're missing a powerful form of leverage. As a result, their impact is severely reduced, and they may end up burning out when they lack the time and energy to focus on what they excel at. By acting this way, they're doing a disservice, not only to themselves, but also to the world.

To conclude, reaching uncommon success and impacting the world requires you to believe that "everything is learnable." This entails adopting the following beliefs:

- I can improve.
- I'm not good enough *yet*, but I inevitably will be.
- I am an unstoppable learner.
- I ask for help whenever I need to.

Meta-Belief #3—Every problem is solvable

Extraordinary people are extraordinary problem-solvers. They find solutions to "impossible" problems and are able to do "impossible" things. Note that every problem is solvable because if it is not, then it isn't a problem, it's just *reality* and must be accepted as such. Therefore, by definition, for every problem, there *must* be a solution of some kind.

Sub-belief #1—I can figure things out

Believing every problem is solvable involves adopting the belief that you can find a solution. No matter what you face, you decide that you *will* find an answer to the challenge. You'll do anything in your power to find the best solutions. Then, you'll act until you resolve the issue at hand.

Life is a never-ending stream of problems, some minor, others major. People committed to doing the extraordinary continuously focus on their vision and how to make it a reality. They think bigger and tackle bigger problems so that they can have a larger impact. You, too, can solve bigger problems. The greater the problems you solve, the bigger your impact on the world will be.

Consequently, instead of asking "Why do bad things happen to me?", enter problem-solving mode and ask yourself, "What am I going to do about it?" Because, to quote the late business philosopher, Jim Rohn, *"It's not what happens that determines the major part of your future, the key is what you do about it."*

Believe in your ability to figure things out. Then, act accordingly.

Sub-belief #2—There are people who have answers to my questions

To solve big issues, believe that there are people who have the answers to your questions. Most of what you're trying to do, others have done before. Learn from them. Soak up their knowledge. If others can do it, you can too. If others can solve big challenges, you can too. Adopt the belief that everything is solvable and avoid:

- Playing the victim,
- Isolating yourself and worrying for days on end, and
- Becoming helpless.

Instead, seek help. Look for people who have solved similar issues in the past. And remind yourself of the following:

- I can figure things out, and
- There are people who have answers to my questions.

Remember, everything is possible. Everything is learnable. Everything is solvable. Make these statements your daily mantras. Let them consume you. Drill them into your mind. Once you internalize these beliefs, you will ignite the fire required to tap into your extraordinary potential.

In **Part II. Applying extreme leverage—1. Thinking**, we'll explore in greater depth how to strengthen your beliefs and make them part of your identity.

Next, we will consider another tool to help you take further control of your mind and reclaim your power.

* * *

Action steps

Start ingraining the Meta-Beliefs below into your mind by completing the corresponding exercises in your action guide:

1. Everything is possible.
2. Everything is learnable.
3. Every problem has a solution.

5

THE POWER OF SUBJECTIVE REALITY

You may believe that to impact the world, you must change the outer world. But before you can transform the outer world, you must transform your inner world. You must first create your own bubble of reality. Then, you must live in it completely. I call it inhabiting your subjective reality.

In a strange sense, you must practice behaving as though you are the only person in the world. You must become the master of your mind and take responsibility for how you think, feel, and act. This is because you are always guaranteed to succeed in changing yourself—at least, to some extent—but you can't guarantee changing others. In truth, we can never know for sure whether others think or feel the same way we do. For all we know, we could be in a game simulation made up of NPCs (non-playable characters). This is why I invite you to consider the following question:

If you were living in a simulation designed to help you learn, grow, and become all you can be, what would you do differently? For instance:

- How would you deal with challenging situations?
- What extraordinary goals would you pursue?

- How would you behave differently?

Another thought experiment is to perceive the world as a mirror reflecting what you put out. Now, if the external world was indeed reflecting your internal world, what would you change within yourself?

For instance:

- What new beliefs would you rely on to navigate the world?
- What excuses and limitations would you let go of?
- What lofty goals would you start pursuing?

You'll discover that the more you act as though your inner thoughts are all that matters, the more power you will gain. As you put the locus of control on yourself (i.e., as you inhabit your subjective world) you'll begin to uncover your true potential. Your main focus will be on:

- Improving the content of your mind by adopting empowering beliefs,
- Learning the skills required to reach your goals, and
- Building your character by cultivating self-discipline, integrity, grit, and so on.

To sum up, when you focus on changing the world, your impact is limited, but when you focus on changing yourself, your overall impact can grow exponentially. Consider this: you can spend your entire life trying to change just one other person and fail, or you can change yourself and impact the lives of countless others.

The concept of subjective reality invites you to claim power over yourself. So, play with it. Act as if you were the only playable character in the world. Behave as though the outside world was a direct reflection of your inner thoughts and feelings. Then, let your subjective reality transform the objective reality around you.

So far, we've seen what assumptions are and how changing them will transform your life. We've discussed the three Laws of Belief and three Meta-Beliefs that you must adopt to become extraordinary. Finally, we've explored the concept of subjective reality and how you can use it to create a more empowering reality. Now that you understand the mindset required to move from ordinary to extraordinary, let's explore what you can do specifically to leverage your impact, multiply your results, and make a difference in the world.

* * *

Action steps

Complete the following exercises using your action guide:

- Close your eyes and imagine that the outside world is merely a projection of your inside world. See yourself as being responsible for the state of the entire world.
- Now, look at areas of your life in which you're not taking full responsibility. Then, complete the following prompt: If I was responsible for the state of the entire world, this is what I would do differently.
- Imagine you're the only playable character in the world. Knowing the world is the reflection of your inner thoughts, what are the most empowering beliefs you could adopt to help you achieve anything you desire? Write down what your beliefs would be.

PART II

APPLYING EXTREME LEVERAGE

As Archimedes said, *"Give me a lever long enough and a fulcrum on which to place it, and I shall move the world."* To impact the world at a grand scale, you must be able to deliver extraordinary results. And extraordinary results require not just an extraordinary mindset, but also, extraordinary leverage. In this part, we'll explore each form of leverage and see how we can use it to explode your impact.

But first, let's briefly define "leverage." In this book, leverage refers to any activity that enables you to increase your impact dramatically. You're just one person so, to impact the world, you inevitably need help. Below are the eight forms of leverage we shall cover:

1. **Thoughts (size and intensity).** Big thoughts create extraordinary leverage. By thinking bigger, you act from a completely different place and, by doing so, you will magnify your impact. And by intensifying your thoughts, you make them more powerful.
2. **Thinking.** Accurate thinking makes each of your decisions far more impactful. The more accurate your model of reality is, the more impactful your actions will be.

3. **Personal growth.** Working on yourself enables you to increase your impact dramatically. Your self-confidence, grit, and relentless desire to learn enables you to attain extraordinary results.
4. **Technologies.** Technology is human labor on steroids. It enables you to multiply time and gather far more energy than you otherwise could. And being able to devote more time and energy to a task means you have more potential power at your disposal.
5. **Focus.** A sustained focus over the long term activates the power of compounding that generates an extraordinary return on the time that you have invested. People often overestimate what they can do in a few months but underestimate what they can accomplish in a few years.
6. **Other people's time/energy.** Your time/energy is limited. Buying other people's time/energy is essential to generating more leverage. It means hiring employees, working with freelancers, or outsourcing part of your business.
7. **Money.** Money (yours or other people's money) is nothing more than stored time and energy. The more money you have, the more time and energy you can use to advance your vision.
8. **Knowledge.** Knowledge is the sum of the progress made by human civilization up until now. It's people's time and energy stored and curated over centuries for its usefulness.

Now, let's review each component of leverage and see how you can use it to increase your impact exponentially.

* * *

Action steps

Using your action guide, rate yourself on your current ability to use each form of leverage to achieve extraordinary results.

1

THOUGHTS (SIZE AND INTENSITY)

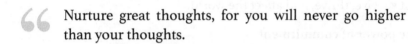 Nurture great thoughts, for you will never go higher than your thoughts.

— BENJAMIN DISRAELI, POLITICIAN AND AUTHOR.

Having bigger thoughts enables us to take impactful actions that will create extraordinary results. Whenever I craft a strategy or work on something, I think big. Doing so makes each of my actions far more impactful. You, too, have the astonishing ability to upgrade the size of your thoughts. And, as you do so, each of your actions will become more impactful.

Acting on big thoughts doesn't necessarily require more energy than acting on smaller ones. In fact, thinking big and going after what you want can energize you far more than pursuing half-baked, minor goals.

What matters most is intent. If you want to take effective action and make a huge impact, the key is to think big and have clear intentions. Put simply, your thoughts act as a reservoir of possibilities that you can tap into. When your reservoir is small, you can select only small, low-impact actions. However, when your reservoir is big, you can choose big, high-impact actions. Increase the size of your reservoir today by thinking bigger.

Thoughts and time

Your thoughts largely determine the future you will create, but there is a time lag between the moment you have a thought and the moment it turns into something tangible. This time lag is both inevitable and necessary. Here's why:

We are eight billion people, each entertaining thousands of thoughts every day. If our thoughts instantly became reality, the world would become even more chaotic. Time acts as a selective mechanism, allowing only specific thoughts to impact the physical world. Think of time as a mechanism that enables you to recommit to important thoughts repeatedly while discarding others. Thoughts given the most attention and infused with strong enough energy are the ones that survive, thrive, and affect the world.

The power of commitment

Thoughts are potential energy. They become powerful only when you commit to them. That is, you must infuse your thoughts with enough energy to make them impactful. People who keep investing their energy in the same empowering thoughts will, over the long term, move closer to the reality they wish to create. Conversely, people who jump from one thought, idea, or project to the next, are unlikely to ever accomplish anything significant.

Now, the following things determine whether and when the intangible (your thoughts) turn into the tangible (actual outcome):

- The size of your thoughts, and
- The intensity of your thoughts.

Let's look at each of these components in turn.

Leverage #1a—Thoughts (size)

 Think big, aim high, act bold. And see just how big you can blow up your life.

— GARRY KELLER, ENTREPRENEUR AND BEST-SELLING AUTHOR.

The operating system on your phone can only ever do what it has been engineered to do. In the same way, your belief system can only ever generate the outcome it was designed for. It won't produce extraordinary results unless you program it to do so. To achieve the impossible for you, you *must* update your operating system.

In all likelihood, you often fail to predict the extreme level of change you can bring within yourself. You probably don't realize to what extent you can disrupt yourself. This is why you must practice thinking bigger. Forget about who you currently are. Instead, start projecting yourself into the future you wish to create. To do this, you must visualize who you could become. Here are a few things you can do to think bigger and avoid reverting to mediocrity:

- Surround yourself with people who set high standards for themselves,
- Consume content from extraordinary people you want to be like,
- Find role models who inspire you in each area of your life, and
- Think bigger, more empowering thoughts, and write statements that you want to be true about yourself, and do so on a daily basis.

Remember, no matter how big you think, you can always think bigger. No matter how much you accomplish, you can always accomplish more. No matter how impossible you think something is for you, it's probably possible.

1) Destroying myths around thinking big

Failing to think big is one of the main reasons that we grow slowly. There are several explanations for this:

1. **We were never taught that we *could* think big.** Nobody ever told us that we can choose to think bigger and raise our standards. It never occurs to us that we can take control of our mind to reach our goals. Therefore, like most people, we've learned to accept our "fate." We've settled for mediocrity and have succumbed to the gravitational pull that moves us toward "average."
2. **We were never taught *how* to think big.** Neither our parents nor our teachers taught us how to use our mind to turn the invisible into the visible. We were never told that between our ears lies the most powerful machine ever created and that, when used properly, our brain can enable us to do "impossible" things.
3. **We believe extraordinary is not for us.** Deep down, we think that while others can achieve extraordinary things, we can't. We see ourselves as being normal, ordinary. And ordinary people cannot become extraordinary. When envisioning our dreams, we focus on the obstacles along the way. We project our current self into the future, and we fail to understand that our future self could be a widely different and better person.

The point is, thinking big is a skill that you can acquire through practice. Big goals may require you to learn new skills, sharpen your focus, and create better strategies, but not necessarily to put in that much more effort. Achieving a ten times bigger vision doesn't require ten times more effort. Making ten times more money doesn't require working ten times harder or ten times longer. We can't exert ten times more effort, but we can think bigger and better—and that is what makes all the difference.

2) How to increase the size of your thinking

To increase the size of your thinking, complete the following exercises:

- **Let go of limitations.** Think of the biggest vision possible. Focus on what you desire for yourself, your family, and the world as a whole. Remember, the stronger your desire, the more likely you are to reach your goal. Aim for what you really want and forget about perceived limitations such as a current lack of skills, resources, talent, network, self-confidence, or discipline (all of which can be overcome).
- **Increase the size of your vision.** Now that you've spent time focusing on developing your compelling vision, make it bigger. What would it look like if you multiply it by ten? Experiment with a level of thinking you've never experienced before. Allow yourself to envision impossible things. Think at the highest level you've ever thought. See how it makes you feel.
- **Further expand your vision.** Now, what would it look like if you multiplied it by one hundred? Notice how you feel. Do you feel uncomfortable? Insecure? Overwhelmed? Anxious? Or do you feel excited, empowered, and alive? Perhaps it's a mix of both.
- **Ask yourself "what if?"** Believe your vision is possible. Ask yourself, "what if?" Why not? Why not me? What if, over time, you could learn any skill and attract any resource you need? Assume that your vision is possible and allow yourself to dream. Let your mind wander into the impossible future you desire. Notice any self-doubt that arises. Observe your self-talk without judging. Practice letting go of your limitations. Spend at least five minutes thinking of "what if."
- **Remind yourself that if someone else can do it, you can, too.** If somebody else has done something before, you can do it too. Let go of the idea that others are smarter than you. Eliminate the belief that you can't learn what you need to learn to reach your goals. Remember, everything is possible.

- **Repeat the process as often as necessary.** Whenever possible, spend time alone thinking bigger thoughts. For instance, you can do so when taking a shower or going for a walk, or when you wake up, or before you go to sleep. In these moments, your mind is more receptive and willing to accept your big thoughts as possibilities. Thinking big is a skill. Practice it—often.

3) "Impossible" is a point of view

Today's impossible is tomorrow's possible. Big thoughts that seem unrealistic today might not be tomorrow. Therefore, instead of reducing your choices to what seems plausible, act as though everything is possible. You will never know what you're capable of achieving until you give it a try. When the founder of SpaceX, Elon Musk, wants to do something, he begins by asking himself the following question:

"Does this break the laws of physics?"

Let that question guide you toward bigger thinking. If something doesn't break the laws of physics, assume it's possible and get moving. For instance, none of the following things break the laws of physics:

- Creating your own business,
- Retiring early, or
- Becoming a millionaire.

And, if you want to think even bigger, neither does becoming a billionaire, eradicating poverty, or dating Beyonce (I didn't say it would be easy). "Impossible" or "unrealistic" don't mean anything by themselves. What I think is possible, you might see as impossible, and vice versa. Things that seem impossible today might be possible tomorrow. This is because who you are today is simply not who you will be tomorrow.

What about you? What do you believe is impossible for you? Now, what would you do if you knew with certainty that it *was* possible, or perhaps even inevitable? Think of all the possibilities.

4) Feeling good vs. doing good

Many people talk big but act small. They are merely trying to look good and feel good by showing how virtuous they are. They say they want to "change the world," "end war." or "eradicate poverty."

But do they? Really?

Their thoughts and actions often tell a different story. Just saying something doesn't make it a reality. Wanting to feel good without having to do anything is another form of instant gratification. It's the same as wanting to become rich without working or wanting to lose weight without changing your diet or your exercise routine. This is an inauthentic, selfish, and lazy way to live life. It's abdicating responsibility and ignoring one's moral obligation to make the best use of one's talents, skills, and personality to contribute to the world.

To impact the world at scale, you must eradicate feel-good activities and destroy any sense of moral superiority. Instead, you must judge yourself on the size and impact of your actions. Ask yourself if your thoughts and actions match your words. Ask yourself if they are likely to produce tangible results.

The point is, thinking big shouldn't be a casual activity. It's not about feeling or looking good. It's *not* about daydreaming or resorting to wishful thinking either. It's committed thinking infused with a genuine desire and a true willingness to make a difference.

5) Purifying your thoughts

The quality of your thoughts will determine the quality of your life. Therefore, improving the quality of your thoughts is the most important work you can ever do. As you change how you think, over time, everything will change for you.

The truth is, you always have a choice. You can entertain beautiful thoughts of compassion, love, and faith. Or you can let thoughts of jealousy, hatred, and anger control your life. The world seems to act like a mirror, reflecting your dominant thoughts back to you. This is why, when you take responsibility for your internal world, the external world begins to change. To become extraordinary, let go of impure and disempowering thoughts and replace them with pure and empowering ones. Remember, your belief system acts as an operating system. If you want to obtain better results, you must upgrade your operating system. To do this you must:

1. Let go of excellent and choose extraordinary.
2. Avoid the pull toward mediocrity.
3. Accept that nobody can see what you see.
4. Eliminate the negative voices inside your head.

Let's go over each of these points.

A. Let go of excellent and choose extraordinary

Extraordinary results require an extraordinary mindset. To impact the world at scale, you must elevate your thoughts beyond the merely excellent. You must keep thinking bigger and bigger, and fight the pull toward mediocrity you face daily.

As you seek to accomplish exceptional things, you'll be tempted to scale back your vision. Self-doubt may creep in. Other opportunities may steal your focus. Friends might tell you to relax. And, before you know it, small thinking will have contaminated your vision. Your job here is to keep your vision pure and unaltered. After all, it is *your* vision, not someone else's. As Gandhi said, "*I will not let anyone walk through my mind with their dirty feet.*" Neither should you. You *must not* let anyone walk all over your vision with their limited and "dirty" thinking.

In short, to accomplish your biggest goals, you must discard "excellent" and move toward "extraordinary." You must guard your mind against the temptations of pursuing half-baked, modest visions. You must continuously recommit to your vision and protect it from any internal attack (a negative mindset) or external attack (other people's thinking). Ultimately, becoming extraordinary is a choice you must make over and over again. This is a life commitment. It's a decision to become the person *you* want to be, not the person other people think you are or want you to be.

B. Avoiding the pull toward mediocrity

By definition, most humans are average people living average lives. Consequently, unless you choose to become extraordinary and design your environment accordingly, you will be pulled back toward the norm, toward mediocrity. The constant pull toward mediocrity is as inevitable as the law of gravity. Below are a couple of examples of how the pull toward mediocrity works:

- Your friends tell you to be "realistic" (i.e., stay average).
- Everyone around you puts you in a box, telling you you're too shy, not smart enough, or lack the discipline to reach your goals.

The point is, as you think big thoughts, people will try to hold you back. This isn't a conscious act. They simply can't help but project their limited perception of reality onto you. Maintaining big thinking will be one of your biggest challenges. It will require daily practice and relentless monitoring. It will demand that you guard your mind against other people's small thinking.

Think of it this way. Your thoughts are the thermostat that regulates your actions. The stronger your thoughts, the higher you set your thermostat. As you raise your thermostat, you start influencing people as opposed to being influenced by them. Your goal should be to reach a point where no event or person in the world can derail you from your path—the point of unbreakable self-confidence.

C. Accepting that nobody can see what you see

So, you've decided you want to impact the lives of millions of people.

Now what?

Here is what will happen: Everybody will tell you it can't be done. They will project onto you their own "reality," their deep-seated fears, and their self-imposed limitations. Accept that reality as being inevitable, but refuse to downgrade your vision to fit in. Your job is to protect your thoughts and prevent anyone from dictating the future you seek to create.

Now, I'm not saying you should reject advice. What I am saying is that what people tell you is often irrelevant, useless, and even harmful. How could it be otherwise, considering that they don't see what you see? Also, since nobody truly understands you, you might not find a mentor or coach. Never use this as an excuse to give up. If there is no obvious existing way, create it. Find role models wherever you can. Then, read everything they wrote. Watch every interview they gave. Do whatever you can to soak up their knowledge and absorb their mindset. "I don't have a mentor" is simply an unacceptable excuse.

To sum up. Upgrade your thinking to match your vision. Don't downgrade it to earn people's validation. Remember, nobody can see what you see. And that's fine because *you* see it clearly and *you* are the master of your reality.

D. Eliminating the negative voices inside your head

You hear voices. And I'm not talking about schizophrenia or other mental illnesses. I'm talking about your internal monologue, your self-talk. Interestingly, your self-talk is not really you talking to yourself. It's voices from the past. It's your mother, your father, your brother, or your teachers. It's the movies you've watched, the books you've read, the songs you've listened to and the conversations you've had.

Most people's inner dialogue is horrendous. They beat themselves up whenever they make a mistake, they blame themselves for past failures, and they compare themselves unfairly with others. Most of the mental suffering people experience is the result of their thinking. They're living in a prison of their own creation. In a sense, they live in their own subjective reality, but this subjective reality is anything but empowering.

As you move toward becoming extraordinary, you must get rid of the negative voices in your head. You must let go of the limitations imposed by your parents, teachers, or society and reconnect with your true self. The following steps will help you do so.

Step #1—Listen to your inner dialogue

The prerequisite to any change is self-awareness. You must know what *is* before you can decide what *could be*. An effective way to identify your limitations is to think of the ideal life you want to create. Imagine you could achieve anything you desire. Then, notice what thoughts arise. Who is talking to you? Is it your mother? Your father? Your brother? Your fifth-grade teacher? And what are they telling you? What limitations are they imposing on you?

In addition, during your day, notice whenever you hear a voice that is not coming from your true self. Try to identify where it originated. By doing so, you'll find out you have many voices inside your head dictating your life and imposing on you a limited version of what your reality could be.

Step #2—Question your thoughts

Your self-talk isn't the truth. It's a story—and it's often a disempowering one. Whenever you notice yourself hearing a limiting belief, ask yourself whether it's true. Then, assume everything is possible and see how false most of your beliefs are. Look for limiting beliefs in the following areas:

- Money
- Relationships
- Success

You probably hold hundreds of limiting beliefs in these areas. Meanwhile, keep working on integrating the following three Meta-Beliefs into your self-talk:

- Everything is possible.
- Everything is learnable.
- Every problem is solvable.

Over time, these Meta-Beliefs will help dissolve many of your limiting beliefs. They will disintegrate disempowering thoughts that have been planted in your mind without your consent.

Step #3—Let go of your negative inner voices

Once you've identified your negative inner voices, practice letting them go. Don't let them limit you and destroy your potential. For most people, the inner voices they hear most are the ones from their parents. In this respect, many people are still living under the influence of their parents—and will do so for their entire lives.

Doing extraordinary things requires you to eliminate the inner voices that define you and confine you. You must allow yourself to break through your limitations to discover your true capabilities. Whenever you find yourself listening to the voices from your past, interrupt your thoughts and remind yourself that everything is possible. Remember, these voices have nothing to do with you and have no real power over you.

You decide what *you* want to do and who *you* want to become.

Instead of remaining stuck in the past, use your imagination to travel into the future you seek to create. Then, act in the present as if everything is possible. Repeat that process as often as necessary. See it as a continuous act of purification of the mind. See yourself shedding layer upon layer of social conditioning and limitations so that you can reconnect with your true self. You wouldn't let other people enter your house with dirty feet, would you? So, stop letting people enter your mind with their dirty thoughts.

Recently, I've noticed that I have many voices in my head, judging me, and telling me what I should and shouldn't do. So, I began to observe them and let them go. For instance:

- There is the voice of my former Korean boss telling me I suck at what I do.
- There is the voice of a former classmate from business school telling me that I'm too ambitious and somewhat delusional.
- There is the voice of my brother telling me that I shouldn't buy a new phone (because I already have one and it's too

expensive). He also tells me I shouldn't invest in courses or in coaching (because I can get everything for free these days).

- There are the voices of acquaintances telling me that I should relax and "enjoy life" instead of polishing my skills and contributing to the world the best I can.

All these voices, and others, impose limits on me. They are not me and I don't have to listen to them. Note that you don't necessarily hear a voice, *per se*. It might be more of a feeling. And that feeling doesn't reflect reality for many reasons.

The bottom line is this. You can choose to be whoever you want to be. Using the Law of Beliefs and Meta-Beliefs, choose to believe anything you want to achieve any goals you have. Get rid of the voices in your head today and rediscover your true self and its extraordinary potential.

Step #4—Optimize your environment

Protecting your mind from the negative influence of people's limited thinking is an endless task. In life, there is a huge gravitational pull toward mediocrity. If you live by default, you will be mediocre. That's why one of the most effective ways to let go of inner voices is to surround yourself physically or virtually with the most positive, empowering, and successful people you can find.

Therefore, continually strive to surround yourself with positive people that inspire you to raise your standards and become better. Find these role models in real life or through books or the internet. Remember that you will fall and rise according to the quality of your thoughts. And, for a major part, your environment will dictate whether you think positive thoughts that serve you or negative thoughts that work against you.

Only you know what you're capable of becoming. As you let go of the voices imposing on you what you can and cannot do, your potential will appear clearer.

Action steps

Complete the corresponding exercises in your action guide.

Leverage #1b—Thoughts (intensity)

 A man cannot directly choose his circumstances, but he can choose his thoughts and so indirectly, yet surely, shape his circumstances.

— JAMES ALLEN, WRITER

Your thoughts contain the seeds of the future that you wish to create, but you must sow the right seeds. Then, you must water them regularly and monitor them closely. A random thought that arises when taking a shower doesn't have the same weight or power as a thought you've been focusing on intentionally for months.

In other words, there is a difference between daydreaming and committed thinking. When you daydream, you merely wish for something to happen. There is no sense of commitment, nor any intensity given to your thoughts. Most people engage in casual thinking most of the time and in most areas of their lives. Such thinking can never create extraordinary results. It has no ability to leave a footprint on your subconscious; it cannot build your desire nor strengthen your commitment. It's nothing more than wishful thinking. And, in life, wishing isn't a strategy, it's a recipe for mediocrity.

On the other hand, *committed* thinking comes with a distinct feeling. Committed thinking is more deliberate, more intense, and more powerful. Through committed thinking, you express your authentic desire for your vision to be realized. It's not wishful daydreaming, but purposeful thinking. When you practice committed thinking, you energize your thoughts and plant the seed for their manifestation. Specifically, practicing committed thinking means:

1. Strengthening your belief, and
2. Intensifying your desire for your vision to come true.

The more intensity you give to your thoughts, the more concrete your vision will be—and the more compelled you will feel to act. Other people may not buy into your vision (yet), but your thoughts will become far more real for you. Furthermore, they will begin to take shape and crystallize in your mind.

1. The size of your thoughts

The size of your thoughts is critical when it comes to making a big impact on your environment. Small thoughts have a small impact while big thoughts offer the potential for a far greater impact. However, big thoughts require far more time and effort before they can impact the world.

For instance, let's say your thought is, "Let's work out today." As the thought arises, you grab your workout gear and head to the gym. In that case, the time lag between your thought and its manifestation is close to zero. Now, imagine you have the thought, "I want to become a doctor." It will take years before it manifests, and you will need to recommit to your goal over and over. Your thought will have to be energizing enough to compel you to take consistent action—i.e., going to classes, studying every day, acing exams, et cetera.

The point is, for big thoughts to come true, you must energize them strongly enough and for long enough to foster the actions required for their manifestation. Now, let's see in detail how to energize your thoughts.

2. Energizing your thoughts

If you simply observe a thought, it has no power. It only gains power when it's energized enough to generate concrete and immediate action. Energizing your thoughts requires that you follow the following four steps:

1. **Understanding the power of thoughts.** This means grasping in depth the mechanism that turns the invisible (thoughts) into the visible (tangible results).
2. **Strengthening your thoughts through repetition.** This means focusing on the same thoughts over and over until they become rock-solid beliefs and change how you feel and act.
3. **Marinating in your thoughts.** This means engaging in committed thinking—i.e., committing to your thoughts over and over with a clear intent and genuine desire to make them come true.
4. **Infusing your thoughts with intense desire.** This means identifying exciting reasons why these thoughts must manifest and thinking of them often.

Now, let's have a closer look at each of these steps in turn.

Step #1—Understanding the power of thoughts

Your thoughts shape your future because they dictate how you act and react in the present. They have the power to turn the intangible into the tangible and make the impossible possible. The first step to intensifying your thoughts is to understand the power of thoughts; it is to realize that what you think about for long enough tends to become your reality. In fact, most of the objects you see around you were once an idea in someone's mind. This idea was infused with a strong enough sense of belief to be turned into reality. You, too, can turn your vision into reality. To impact the lives of millions of people, you must leverage your ability to believe.

Now, there's nothing irrational or mystical about turning invisible thoughts into tangible items. Our thoughts work the same way regardless of our religious beliefs (or lack thereof). Let's see how thoughts become things.

- **First, you have a thought.** You may select that thought or it might arise spontaneously. Note that the most powerful thoughts are often spontaneous; they come to you when your mind is relaxed (when taking a shower, walking, meditating, et cetera).

- **Second, you give that thought your attention.** Once you have identified a thought worth "manifesting," you focus on that thought repeatedly. By doing so, you eventually feel compelled to act to close the gap between where you are and where you want your thought to take you.
- **Third, that thought takes shape.** As you keep giving it your attention and act accordingly, that thought takes shape and becomes your reality.

Let's revisit the earlier example of wanting to find a more meaningful job. Feeling dissatisfied with your job, the thought, "I want to change careers," arises. You decide to entertain that thought. As you give it more attention, you ask yourself questions such as:

- What do I really like to do?
- What job would be ideal for me?
- Who can help me change my career?
- What is the next step?

In other words, as the thought, "I want to change careers," becomes your dominant thought, you've introduced tension. Now you feel the urge to close the gap between where you are and where you want to be (i.e., to eliminate or reduce that tension). Your subconscious begins to work for you, looking for answers and noticing anything that could help you reach your goal.

Soon enough, you feel compelled to act. You update your resume, reflect on what you like and dislike about your job, learn new skills, and meet with headhunters.

By using your thoughts, you've altered your actions and set the universe in motion. What was merely an inconsequential thought is shaping your future. It has taken on a life of its own. You arranged your first job interview. You took a course to learn a useful skill. You met people in the industry that you want to work in. It's just a matter of time before you land the new job you're looking for.

This is how the process of turning your beliefs into reality works. Keep giving a thought your attention and, soon enough, it becomes your dominant thought. Self-doubt begins to disappear. A mere possibility (intangible thought) turns into an inevitability (tangible outcome). To impact millions of people with your actions, you must master this process. You must practice turning what you believe into a reality.

Remember, your ability to believe can never be taken away from you. It can only be forgotten temporarily. Regardless of your circumstances, you can always choose to believe. No matter how many times you fail, you can always choose to get back up and try again. And as you learn to master your beliefs, you rise above your circumstances, achieving the things you once thought impossible.

Step #2—Strengthening thoughts through repetition

Every master is a master of repetition. Martial arts experts practice the same punches thousands of times. Outstanding public speakers rehearse their speeches for days. And accomplished writers, write and rewrite as many times as necessary. Similarly, the master of his or her thoughts thinks empowering thoughts over and over.

When you try to think bigger, it will feel difficult at first. It won't seem realistic. How can you do something you've never done before? You may not know how, or you may lack the necessary skills or resources (right now). But what ultimately prevents you from doing "impossible" things is merely a lack of belief.

Your thoughts act as a limiting factor. Self-doubt paralyzes you. Deep down, you don't believe you can do it. This is why you must use the power of repetition to internalize empowering beliefs such as "Everything is possible."

How to use repetition to strengthen your thoughts

One major reason people fail to reach their goals is lack of consistency. In life, what matters most is not what you do every other day, it's what you do *every day*. The repetition of simple daily habits over a long period of time turns ordinary people into extraordinary achievers. And beliefs are nothing more than habits in thinking. In other words, beliefs are thoughts that have crystallized over time through the power of repetition.

As the motivational speaker, Zig Ziglar, once said, *"People often say that motivation doesn't last. Well, neither does bathing—that's why we recommend it daily."* Well, thoughts don't last either. It's only through repetition that you can make them permeate your mind and become part of your core beliefs.

The point is, to strengthen your thoughts you must repeat them daily. You must immerse yourself in an empowering environment, full of empowering people. You must feed your mind with the beliefs that will enable you to accomplish anything you can imagine. To crystallize your thoughts, I encourage you to do the following:

1) Consume positive content daily

You can easily lose confidence, and you will likely "relapse" many times in your journey toward cultivating extraordinary self-belief. The less inspiring your environment is, the tougher it will be to hold onto empowering beliefs. Consequently, make sure you consume inspirational and educational content daily. The blogger, Steve Pavlina, explained how he changed his mindset, exploded his productivity, and aced university by listening to educational audiobooks for hours daily. Personally, I've absorbed an incredible amount of personal development resources over the years and still avidly do so. I've read the classics multiple times and listened to some audiobooks dozens of times.

Remember, to do the impossible and make a real difference, you must do uncommon things average people won't do. Consume positive content daily and begin to reprogram your mind for extraordinary success. And, more importantly, take massive action to move you toward your goals.

2) Write down affirmations

Affirmations are statements we use to affirm who we are or who we desire to be. We repeat affirmations all day long, silently in our mind or when interacting with others. In fact, our inner self-talk is a never-ending playlist of affirmations. And, unfortunately, these affirmations are often quite negative.

- "Why did I do that? I'm so stupid."
- "I'm just not good enough."
- "Other people have it easy."
- "I can't do it."

By practicing positive affirmations, you select the beliefs you want to implant in your mind. In short, you switch off the autopilot. Remember, affirmations are merely tools you use to affirm who you want to be. Every day, practice writing down affirmations that will help you reach your goals. For instance, the entrepreneur, Tom Bilyeu, has a set of beliefs he likes to repeat to himself, such as:

- You can do anything you set your mind to without limitations.
- Human potential is nearly limitless.
- Any obstacle can be overcome.

These are great general affirmations but I like to personalize mine, such as:

- I can learn anything I want faster than almost anybody else in the world.
- There is no limit to what I can do, be, have, and become.
- I can always improve.

As you keep practicing affirmations, over time you can personalize them using words or sentences you resonate with the most.

The bottom line is, you can either let affirmations run on autopilot and control your life, or you can select specific affirmations and repeat them for long enough until they change your belief system and transform your life.

How to use affirmations effectively

There are many ways to use affirmations, but I encourage you to write them down daily using pen and paper. I write mantras and affirmations each day and change them based on my mood and what I want to focus on that day. Here are examples of mantras and affirmations I write:

Mantras/principles:

- Make today count.
- Appreciate everything and everyone in my life.
- Share more of myself with the world. Be more authentic.
- Love more. Care more. Listen more. Be more compassionate. Lighten the whole world with my smile and my attitude.
- Do what makes me feel proud of myself.
- Be brave. Be courageous.
- Test my limits. Do the impossible.
- Focus on the process.
- Become better every day.
- Try harder. Go the extra mile.

Affirmations:

- Everything is possible.
- I can achieve any goal I set my mind to without limitations.
- I'm extraordinary at everything I do.

Now, to start changing your beliefs, you can do the following:

- Repeat affirmations each day.
- Observe your self-talk and continuously strive to replace disempowering statements with empowering ones.
- Rephrase your self-talk whenever you catch yourself being too critical. Make it more self-compassionate. Remember this universal truth: we always do the best we can with what we have, based on what we know *at the time*. If we could have done better, we would have.

3) Think of your core beliefs during the day

Whatever you think about most of the time, you tend to become. To internalize positive beliefs, think of them during the day. Think of the three Meta-Beliefs whenever you are taking a shower, going for a walk, after you wake up each morning, or when you go to bed each evening. For instance:

- **Assume everything is possible.** Envision yourself achieving all the things you've ever dreamed of. Meanwhile, know that if you build a strong enough desire and take consistent action, many of your goals will become a reality. Observe how it makes you feel. If limiting beliefs, worries, or feelings of self-doubt creep in, suspend them temporarily. Then, refocus on your dreams and feel the inevitability of their realization.

- **Imagine everything is learnable.** Repeat to yourself the belief that everything is learnable. Then, think of the concrete implications. What specific skills will you acquire? And how do you feel, knowing that you will inevitably learn those skills? Remind yourself that if someone else can achieve something remarkable, you can too. Reconnect with the unstoppable learner within yourself. And remember that you can learn any skill you need to reach any goal you have in any area you desire.

- **Remind yourself that every problem has a solution.** Realize that there are many people who have solved similar problems before. Understand that you are not alone and that there are people who have the solution to your challenge. Trust your ability to figure things out. Ask for help when you need it. Perceive yourself as an extraordinary problem-solver and see yourself acting accordingly.

Beliefs are thinking habits. Make sure you focus on your empowering beliefs every day until they become a habit. Then, act accordingly. As you act and build a track record of success, your beliefs will further solidify. Notice how your thoughts and actions both feed your beliefs and create a virtuous cycle. That is:

1. Thinking the same thought creates a strong belief.
2. That strong belief compels you to act.
3. As you act, you further strengthen that belief.
4. As that belief strengthens, it generates more positive thoughts.
5. These thoughts further strengthen your belief.

Or, to simplify:

thoughts —> beliefs —> actions —> beliefs —> thoughts

For instance, let's say you decide to adopt the belief that "everything is learnable." As a result:

1. You keep reminding yourself that everything is learnable, which strengthens your belief over time.
2. You are compelled to learn something new that you didn't dare to learn before (or merely dabbled with). It could be learning to play an instrument, studying a foreign language, or acquiring a practical skill.
3. As you persevere and see early results, your belief that everything is learnable strengthens.
4. Now, you begin to have more thoughts such as, "What else could I learn?"
5. As a result, your belief that "everything is learnable" becomes even stronger.

Bear in mind that your beliefs will only become strong when you repeat them often and act accordingly in a consistent manner. Become the master of your beliefs by strengthening them every day. What you believe, you will eventually become.

Step #3—Marinating in your thoughts

Your thoughts grow in intensity to the extent that you focus on them. You must think the same thoughts repeatedly until they consume you. You must allow your thoughts to incubate and grow within you. To do so, spend time bathing in the reality that you seek to create. Marinate your thoughts until they harden in your mind. Below are specific things you can do to crystallize your thoughts.

1) Embracing alone time

If you want to impact the lives of millions of people, you must grow accustomed to spending a lot of time alone. Spending time by yourself enables you to:

- **Clarify your vision.** Clarity isn't something that happens only once. It's an ongoing process that requires constant fine-tuning. Spending time by yourself enables you to refine your vision. I encourage you to use a pen and paper and write down what you want on a regular basis.
- **Create opportunities.** The more time you spend alone thinking of your vision, the more your subconscious will find solutions to realize it. Ask yourself questions such as, "Who can help me reach that goal?", "What's the best strategy?", or "What skills do I need to develop?" What you seek, seeks you. When you know what you want and act accordingly, many opportunities will appear.
- **Strengthen your conviction.** As you give your vision your attention and infuse it with a sense of commitment, it will grow on you. Your conviction will strengthen and, as a result, people will be unable to dissuade you from pursuing your dream. In other words, the more you spend time alone marinating in your vision, the stronger it will become. What was once an idea will become a possibility and, over the long term, an inevitability.

Remember, nobody can truly understand your vision. It's *your* responsibility to clarify it, strengthen it, and protect it. You do that by spending a disproportionate amount of time by yourself thinking about it, by marinating in it until it takes on a life of its own.

2) Overcoming self-doubt

Big dreams and ambitious visions scare us. We tend to think:

- Why do I even dare to dream that big?
- Who am I to deserve such an incredible life?
- With so many people who are smarter, better, or work harder, how will I even get there?

As you think bigger thoughts, you will face self-doubt and that's okay. Just because you have negative thoughts doesn't mean that they will turn into reality. Simply allow your thoughts to exist. Remember, what matters most is the specific thoughts you energize through intense desire and strong commitment. Over time, the thoughts you pay attention to will grow. Meanwhile, the thoughts you allow to exist and observe with detachment will wither away. Just keep marinating in the thoughts that will enable you to design the life you desire most.

3) Having faith in your vision

At first, your vision will seem unrealistic. Don't worry. This is normal. Fortunately, you don't need to know yet exactly how you'll reach your goals. You merely need to know why. The more reasons you have to reach your goal, the more energized your thoughts will become, and the more emotional these reasons are the better. When you want something badly enough, your goals start moving toward you more than you move toward them. And, as you act, the path ahead will become clearer.

Marinate in your vision. Let your mind wander into the future that you desire. Whatever you want to come true, be there in your mind years before it happens. This is the starting point to achieving extraordinary results.

4) Accepting loneliness

As you move toward your vision, you will feel lonely at times. People will misunderstand you or doubt you. They may even ridicule you.

Accept it.

You won't achieve extraordinary results by listening to ordinary people. Extraordinary people harden themselves in solitude. They use their "alone time" to refine their vision and purify their minds from external negativity. They refuse to let others impose limitations on them. By relentlessly recommitting to their vision, they build an impenetrable shield around it and guard themselves against the mediocrity of the world.

Use your alone time to focus on your vision. Keep refining it and continually strengthen your level of conviction. What people think you can or cannot do is irrelevant. The only thing that matters is what you think about yourself and your abilities. Note that, in the process toward generating extraordinary results, you may have to let go of current friends and acquaintances. Two simple questions to ask yourself are, "Is this relationship helping me become a better version of myself? Does it move me closer to my goals and to the person I aspire to become?"

Step #4—Strengthen your thoughts through desire

The major obstacle between you and your vision is a lack of desire. Desire is what gives intensity to your thoughts and drives you to keep moving despite the inevitable setbacks. Personally, I've achieved most of the goals I had a strong desire for. Conversely, I failed to reach most of the goals I lacked a desire for. Look at your own life and you will realize the same is likely true for you too. To move closer to your vision, you *must* build a strong desire. Then, you must be able to sustain that desire over an extended period of time. Now, let's see what you can do specifically to build desire.

How to build desire

We all have different desires. We feel the urge to pursue certain goals. Or circumstances lead us to feel strongly about specific issues. But whatever initial desire we may have, it won't be enough. The excitement we feel at the outset of a new venture won't last. The high we may receive from reading this book will quickly fade away as well. When confronted with the harsh reality, sooner or later, excitement will dissipate, and desire will wither away. This is why we must build our desire muscle and make it stronger so that it lasts longer. We must make it a habit like brushing our teeth or going to the gym. With a strong enough desire sustained over the long term, there are almost no limits to what we can accomplish.

The 3 step-method to cultivate desire

Desire is at the origin of most accomplishments in this world. To strengthen your desire, follow the steps below:

1. Uncover your desires through authenticity (Identify).
2. Strengthen your desires through specificity (Build).
3. Maintain your desires through practice (Maintain).

Step #1—Uncover your desires through authenticity (Identify)

A. Fully embrace your ambitions

Many people are ashamed of their ambitions. They believe being too ambitious is bad. They think, "Who do I think I am to believe I deserve that?", or "I should be content with what I have." By doing so, they deny the burning desire within, they sell themselves short, and they say "no" to their dreams and to the person they could become. Truth is, no one but you can ever tell you what you should do with your life, let alone who you should become.

Many people struggle to build desire because they believe they can't have what they want and shouldn't go after it. As a result, they settle for more "realistic" goals. But desire is born from chasing what you want while becoming the person capable of achieving it. Half-baked goals only lead to weak desire. They don't inspire you to improve your skills, harden your mind, or become the best version of yourself.

I'm not interested in just making a living with my books. I want to sell tens of millions of books. I want to become the best writer that I can possibly be. I want to work with extraordinary people who want to do extraordinary things. I want to test the limits of what is possible for me. And even though I will never reach my full potential—no one ever does—I want to feel wonderful for having tried. So, I'm not apologizing for being ambitious or for wanting to live my life to the fullest. And why should I?

What about you? Will you keep shying away from being extraordinary? Will you keep apologizing for having lofty dreams and beautiful aspirations? Will you let the world decide who you're going to be, or will *you* decide who you're going to be and let the world adjust accordingly?

The bottom line is this. Extraordinary results start with the willingness to accept the extraordinary power within yourself. It begins when you allow yourself to think big and go after what you *really* want. Note that any goal is merely a dream with a deadline. You might not reach your ultimate vision, but you can always break it down into smaller goals. So, embrace your vision fully. Allow yourself to think big. Then, take the first step. This will build more desire than anything else you can ever do.

B. Gain clarity regarding who you want to become

One of my favorite quotes is the following by Jim Rohn:

"Success is not to be pursued; it is to be attracted by the person you become."

What matters most isn't who you are today or who you were yesterday, but who you will become tomorrow. To strengthen desire, you must gain clarity regarding who you want to become. You can't get excited about vague goals or fuzzy visions. You must develop a sense of the kind of person you aspire to become.

This is why you must pursue goals that matter to *you*. Remember that having genuine excitement is the doorway to outstanding achievements. The value of a goal or vision doesn't lie in achieving it. It lies in the person you become *while moving toward it*. Your vision is merely a tool that helps you become more than you were. And strong desire is the main driver that will guide you along the way.

C. Identify the whys behind your goals or vision

Once you set compelling goals, strengthen your desire by exploring the reasons behind your goals—the whys. When you have enough whys, the how will take care of itself. Your whys can be of different natures, but they must touch you deeply. The stronger the emotions, the better. To stay motivated, use the following four types of motivators.

Motivator #1—Ego

Have you ever worked hard so that you could prove naysayers wrong? Have you ever done anything to make your parents proud? Have you ever tried to impress someone you like? If so, you know how to use ego in a positive way—to strengthen your desire.

Ego is simply our desire to enhance our sense of self through external validation—making our parents proud, proving naysayers wrong, becoming famous, et cetera. It can be a powerful agent for change. I have used it myself to attain many of my goals. I've worked hard to make my parents proud of me and to prove that people who didn't believe in me were wrong.

Now, while ego is a powerful motivator, it should be used carefully and sparingly. When you act out of ego, your focus tends to be on the external world. You become obsessed with how others perceive you. Or you want to gather resources, become famous or accumulate wealth. Ego comes from a place of insecurity and inadequacy. This is why, as you grow, you want to rely less on ego and more on motivators such as love.

Motivator #2—Love

Love is another powerful motivator. By love, I mean a sincere desire to contribute to the world. We're often happier when our focus is on helping others. For instance, we feel good when we:

- Compliment someone,
- Give money to charities, or
- Volunteer to help people in need.

We all have an innate desire to be useful and serve others, or at least, I like to believe most of us do. Love—our desire to contribute to the world selflessly—is an extraordinarily powerful motivator. When we embrace our desire to make a difference, we feel a surge of motivation.

Think about it. Why do most wealthy people still work? Wouldn't they be better off sipping cocktails on the beach? They keep working because being useful to others is what gives us our humanity. When we delude ourselves into believing we can opt out of society, we experience a lack of motivation. This is merely a signal for us to return to work and share more of ourselves with the world.

The point is, to build desire, embrace your drive to contribute to the world in your own way, whether it's educating the new generations, cleaning the environment, helping people learn languages, or becoming the best parent that you can be.

So, in what way do you want to contribute to the world? If you could only leave one thing, idea, or product behind after you passed away, what would it be?

Motivator #3—Fear

Yet another powerful motivator is fear. By fear, I mean the desire to move away from what we don't like (e.g., a toxic environment, unhealthy habits, poor relationships, negative emotions).

Fear is good. It drives us to move away from what we don't want. It creates emotional suffering, and when the suffering becomes unbearable, drastic changes become manageable. For instance, fear:

- Makes us eat healthily and exercise to avoid becoming sick,
- Motivates us to look for a partner to avoid living alone, and
- Drives us to upgrade our skills to earn a promotion so that we can take better care of our family.

Years ago, I was an unhappy employee. When at work, I kept looking at the clock on the office wall, hoping time would pass faster. I couldn't envision myself staying at the same job for the rest of my life.

The fear of being stuck in a soul-destroying job instead of using my skills to impact the world became too much. Things had to change, and this became a huge motivator.

Now, think of your own situation. How can you use fear to strengthen your desire to change and become more than you currently are?

Motivator #4—Desire

Another motivator is desire. Most of us have a natural desire to do and become more. The more you can reconnect to that innate desire, the better. To help you do so, consider the following questions:

- What are you thinking about when you get excited? What do you think about when taking a shower? Where does your focus go when you're taking a walk? Notice whenever you feel a sense of excitement and possibility. What can you learn about yourself and your dreams?
- What excites you? What do you want out of life? For example, do you want to travel the world? Speak multiple languages? Become a world-class speaker? What can you infer regarding your areas of interest?
- What are you naturally drawn toward? What activities do you engage in when left alone? Are you into building stuff? Reading biographies? Studying languages? What does this say about you, your natural talent and your innate desires?
- What do you want to change in the world? What issues are closest to your heart? How does this align with your values?

Find your innate desire. Then tap into it. This is the key to growing and becoming the person you aspire to be.

D. Strengthen your whys

To further strengthen your desire, identify your motivators—your whys. Make them specific and write them down. Writing is a powerful way to crystallize your thoughts and organize your mind. For each motivator, come up with compelling reasons to reach your vision. Let's go over a few examples using the four motivators discussed previously:

Ego:

Let's say you want to make your parents proud of you. Why is that exactly? How would you articulate that desire? For instance, it could be:

- My mother left her job to raise me, and I'm grateful for that.
- My parents always believed in me, and I don't want to disappoint them.
- I was never good enough for my father, so I'm going to be the best version of myself that I can be, and I'll show him how great I am.

Reflect on your own life. How can you use ego to strengthen your desire?

Love:

What's your unique way to contribute to the world? What does it mean for you to express yourself to the fullest?

Identify what contribution you'd like to make and how you would feel as a result. Be specific. For me, it would look like this:

- I want people to realize how much power they have to change their lives by changing how they think.
- I want my readers to believe in themselves and use their minds to achieve things that they thought were impossible.
- I want my readers to set extraordinary visions and impact the lives of millions of people.

Your turn now. What's your unique way to express yourself and contribute to the world?

Fear:

What are you afraid of? What do you need to do to overcome your fears? And what will happen if you do nothing? Project yourself ten to twenty years into the future and see the consequences.

For instance, some fears could be:

- I don't want to stay at the same boring job for the rest of my life.
- I don't want to die with regrets.
- I don't want to become sick.

What about you? How can you use fear-based motivation to strengthen your desire and help you move toward your most exciting goals?

Desire:

What are you drawn toward? What do you desire? What thoughts excite you the most?

Notice when you feel excitement. Identify the thoughts you're having as you do so. Then, elaborate. For example, perhaps you want to travel, be the best in your field, or become a polyglot. Now, why do you desire these things? What would they do for you? How would they help the wider world?

Why exactly do you want to travel more? It could be that you want to try exotic dishes, take pictures of breathtaking scenery, or meet with locals to learn about their culture.

Why exactly do you want to be the best in your field? It could be to feel good about yourself, to make your family proud of you, or to make money so that you can provide for your family and give more to charity.

Why exactly do you want to become a polyglot? Perhaps you simply love learning languages. Or perhaps you enjoy connecting with people in their native language, which helps you understand their culture better.

To conclude, by using the four motivators, you can generate an incredible amount of motivation and cultivate a strong desire to move forward with your goals. And with a strong enough desire, almost any goal you envision becomes possible.

Bear in mind that your main motivators are likely to change over time. Ideally, you want to move from ego- and fear-based motivators to love- and desire-based behaviors. But don't judge yourself for acting out of ego or fear to begin with. We all do this.

Step #2—Strengthen your desire through specificity (Build)

Stack your whys

By now, you should have several reasons for reaching your goals. Let's add more. To do so, come up with as many compelling reasons as you can to strengthen your desire. Then, identify which motivator(s) they rely on the most. The more compelling reasons you have to reach your goals, the more likely you are to do so.

More specifically, to stack your whys, do the following:

- **List all the reasons you have to reach your goals.** Write down all the reasons you can think of, whether big or small.
- **Make them specific.** Your brain loves specificity. Add details. Don't just say why you want something. Write down how it will make you feel. Visualize where you will be and what you will be doing when you reach your goal. Create a concrete situation or scene in your mind. In a sense, remember the future. That is, visualize it as if it was a memory from the past rather than a fuzzy dream.
- **Read your list.** Then, go through your list and stack all your whys in your mind. Amplify them. Combine them. Practice strengthening your desire to move toward your vision.

Remember, as with anything else, building desire is a skill. You can actively learn to strengthen your desire. And, once you've done that, the next step is to maintain it over the long term so that you will inevitably move closer to your vision each and every day.

Step #3—Maintain your desire through practice (Maintain)

Now that you've started strengthening your desire, you want to maintain it over the long term to help you feel motivated to act toward your vision.

To maintain desire long term, you can do the following things:

1. Find inspiring models,
2. Consume inspirational content daily,
3. Take daily actions, and
4. Remind yourself of your whys on a consistent basis.

A. Find inspiring role models

What someone else can do, you most likely can too. This is why, nothing is more inspiring than seeing another person doing extraordinary things.

Role models are living proof of what's possible. They show us the way toward our impossible vision. They act as a mirror that reflects to us the future self we could become. The glass may still need to be polished, but underneath layers of dirt—worries, limitations, fears, and insecurities—we can catch a glimpse of our potential.

The role models we are drawn to also reflect to us our deepest values and aspirations. They can be the beacon of hope that we need when in doubt. Whatever you want to accomplish, remember that there are people who have already done similar things. Gain inspiration from them. Imitate them. Meanwhile, keep working on finding your authentic voice so that you can become someone else's role model too.

Since role models make the impossible look possible, they have the power to turn your weak and insecure thoughts into rock-solid beliefs that will change your life. Every time I find inspiring people, I buy the books they've written or watch the videos they've recorded. But, more importantly, I strive to act on their advice so that I can, over time, achieve similar results.

Take a moment to think of the role models you look up to.

How to identify good role models

You can find role models in any area of your life, and you can have as many as you want. For instance, you can have role models in your:

- Career,
- Diet,
- Finance,
- Health,
- Hobbies,
- Mindset, and
- Relationships.

Ask yourself the following questions:

Who has the career I dream of? Who has the intimate relationship I'd love to have? Who has the financial abundance I want to create? Who has the extraordinary mindset I want to cultivate? Who has developed the strength of character I aspire to build?

Start noticing whenever you find someone inspiring. It could be when listening to a podcast or reading a book. Or it could be someone you meet in the real world. In the same way CEOs have a board of administration, create your own board of advisors. That is, build your portfolio of role models. At first, they may be people you have never met. But, over time, you can develop an actual network of people to support you. For instance, one of my friends is knowledgeable about health. So, I contact him whenever I have a health-related question. In fact, whenever I have an issue, my first question is always, "Who can help me answer it?"

Note that you don't need to like everything about a role model. Take what inspires you and leave the rest. For instance, someone may be successful in business but have a terrible relationship with his or her family. If so, aim to absorb the strategies and mindsets that they use to achieve business success. For other areas, look somewhere else.

B. Consume inspirational content daily

When you stop moving toward your goals, you lose momentum, your desire decreases, and your confidence diminishes. This is why you must cultivate desire daily.

When I started writing, I was struggling. The number of visitors on my blog was abysmal, sales of my books didn't even cover my expenses, and many acquaintances didn't believe in me. Unsurprisingly, I fell prey to self-doubt. However, I knew that remaining optimistic and staying focused on the process for a reasonably long period of time was key to achieving anything I wanted. So, I kept writing. Daily. And I kept my desire alive. Specifically, to stay motivated, every day I:

- Watched motivational videos,
- Read inspirational books,
- Practiced gratitude, and
- Kept working on my business.

I looked for role models too. I read posts from authors making six or seven figures a year. I took screenshots of their yearly sales and put them in a folder on my computer. I sought out successful authors in my field and dissected everything they did. I wanted to make sure I had the best strategy possible.

C. Take daily action

Extraordinary results come from effective processes when they are repeated consistently. What you do every single day compounds over time and creates outstanding results. Below are some benefits of daily actions:

- **They generate incredible momentum.** When you act daily, you begin to build motivation. Daily action stimulates your creativity, keeps you engaged and nurtures your dreams.
- **They build self-confidence.** When you move toward your vision each day, you boost your confidence and start believing that your vision is possible.

- **They give you constant feedback.** The more action you take, the more opportunities you have to adjust your trajectory, refine your strategy, and eventually reach your destination.

The bottom line is this. Focusing on what you do daily is key to building and maintaining desire and keeping your dreams alive. And with the right process, you can achieve almost anything you desire. For instance:

- Dedicate an hour each day to finding your life partner and you will eventually succeed.
- Exercise daily and you'll reap the rewards over the long term.
- Spend time learning a language daily and you will eventually become fluent.

D. Remind yourself of your whys on a consistent basis

Finally, to cultivate desire, recall all the compelling reasons behind your vision. Keep envisioning your ideal future. Notice the reasons that appeal the most to you. Are they ego-based? Fear-based? Desire-based? Love-based? Whatever your answer is, it's fine. The key is that you feel motivated to move closer to your vision.

Let me repeat it: The intensity of your desire is the single most important factor when it comes to achieving anything you want. When your desire is strong enough and kept alive for long enough, you're more likely to reach whatever goals you envision.

To conclude, desire is a habit. You either cultivate it each day and strengthen its intensity, or you let it wither away, and you lose momentum. You may even begin to feel sorry for yourself. Desire is the tool through which you express your unique personality and imprint it on the world around you. Cultivate desire. Then, express yourself and share more of who you are.

* * *

Action steps

Complete the corresponding exercises in your action guide.

2

THINKING

 You should take the approach that you're wrong. Your goal is to be less wrong.

— ELON MUSK, ENTREPRENEUR.

Your ability to think well is critical. It's all the truer when you seek to impact the world. Accurate thinking is a powerful lever that can enable you to scale your impact massively. *By thinking more accurately, you can create effective strategies that, in turn, will help you take impactful actions.*

1. The power of accurate thinking

By striving to think accurately, you begin to perceive the world as it is, not as you wish it to be. You start recognizing patterns in the human mind. You become aware of the cognitive biases that lead people to make poor decisions and take ineffective action.

The truth is this. The human brain is a pattern recognition device. It makes sense of the information around us by identifying patterns. However, this mechanism is far from perfect. Our brain continuously makes assumptions and takes shortcuts. While this enables us to consume less energy—which, historically, has increased our chance of surviving and reproducing—it also causes us to make inaccurate assumptions. We make hypotheses, see correlations, and assume causations where none exist. Our biases prevent us from seeing reality as it is and making correct decisions.

Despite all my efforts, I still make poor assumptions. I judge people based on their looks, the clothes they wear, or the career they choose. I also misread situations, trying to guess people's intentions—and often get it horribly wrong. My point is, we make inaccurate assumptions all the time, which is why we must work hard to improve our thinking.

1) Improving your model of reality

A model of reality is a set of assumptions and beliefs we hold about ourselves or the world around us. It's how we perceive the world. And because we all have different upbringings, genes, circumstances, and life experiences, no two people have the identical model.

Now, why is your model of reality important? Because it determines how you think and navigate this world. The more accurate your model is, the more powerful your actions will be. Conversely, if your model is flawed, you'll fail to obtain any significant results no matter how hard you try.

Therefore, to achieve extraordinary results, you must work relentlessly on refining your model of reality. The closest your model of reality is to actual reality, the more you can impact the world. This is because, every single decision you make places them on top of a solid foundation (i.e., an accurate model of reality). In short, you're interacting with the world as it *is* rather than *as you wish it to be*.

Many people fail in life because they rely on ineffective strategies. They fall for get-rich-quick schemes, jump from one trendy diet to the next, or act on tips they read online, hoping for the best. Unfortunately, it doesn't work. A sound strategy is the prerequisite to extraordinary results. With great strategies, empowering beliefs, and compelling whys, almost any goal is achievable over the long term.

To sum up, humans have an inherent desire to make sense of the world around us. We hate uncertainty. Therefore, we keep making assumptions. We want to believe we understand how the world works. We're convinced our political or religious beliefs are correct, but we're often wrong. Thus, be extra careful with your assumptions. Question each one of them and develop solid hypotheses to create effective strategies, not hypotheses based on a foundation of sand.

2) Strategy vs. tactics

Too many people go through life relying on a bunch of tactics to reach their goals. Unfortunately, tactics can never create extraordinary results unless they are part of a well-thought-out strategy. Now, let me explain the difference between strategy and tactics. It's a major one. Put simply:

- A strategy is a plan of action you use to reach a specific goal.
- A tactic is a specific action or method that belongs to a larger strategy.

A strategy relies on different tactics that, when put together, create a coherent set of actions. This coherent set of actions creates tangible results. Now, here is what most people do: they use a mix of tactics they've read online or learned from friends. The problem is, putting a bunch of tactics together doesn't make for a strategy. You don't throw random ingredients together hoping to create a Michelin-star meal. That is, there must be a clear logic behind every action you take. There must be a coherent set of actions that belong to a larger strategy.

A strategy gives you a solid foundation, a framework to make decisions. For instance, a strategy might be to:

- Offer the cheapest product with low margin but high volume.
- Focus on high quality and only serve a small segment of the market.
- Serve only a specific type of customer.

- Sell your products online only with no physical stores.
- Use franchises to expand your business.

Now, let me give you some specific examples of strategies.

McDonald's

Most people think that McDonald's is in the business of selling burgers. But that's not really the case. At least, that's not how they make the majority of their money. McDonald's is mostly a real estate company. Among the close to 40,000 stores that it operates worldwide, about eighty-five percent are franchises. McDonald's makes money by collecting rent from each franchise. In addition, it generates revenue by buying and selling properties via its real estate subsidiary. In fact, most of its profits come from the rent it collects (around eighty percent).

Thanks to its real estate strategy, McDonald's is able to protect itself against the ups and downs of the fast-food business.

Tesla

Many people see Tesla as a car company. But is it? While most of the money it currently makes comes from selling cars, in truth, Tesla is more of a software/technology company. Tesla's strategy is quite simple (but *not* easy). For its CEO, Elon Musk, "*The pace of innovation is all that matters in the long run.*" While the legendary investor, Warren Buffet, is in love with barriers to entry and moats, Elon Musk considers that the only true sustainable "moat" is the pace of innovation, that is, being able to innovate faster than any other company. Believing that the pace of innovation is all that matters, Tesla can focus all of its energy on innovation and does so as fast as it possibly can.

Southeast Airlines

Thanks to a clear strategy that guides all its decisions, Southeast Airlines is one of the world's most profitable airlines, and it has been for a long time. They aren't trying to appeal to all passengers. Instead, they focus entirely on offering low-cost flights.

The bottom line is, by having a strategy, we can identify what to do, and perhaps even more importantly, what *not* to do. An overarching strategy makes the decision-making process easier and allows us to channel our energy and the energy of others effectively. And our ability to accumulate energy and channel it in the right direction is key to maximizing our impact.

What about you? Do you know exactly what you're trying to do? Are you working from a Michelin-star recipe or are you merely throwing a bunch of ingredients together hoping for the best?

2. Overcome thinking biases

As much as we'd like to think we're rational, we are in fact emotional. We tend to act based on emotions and then rationalize our decisions afterward. To think accurately, you must overcome many cognitive biases. You can't become extraordinary by thinking poorly. In this section, we'll go over the main thinking biases that you must be aware of to improve your thinking skills, namely:

1. Sunk cost fallacy.
2. Correlation and causation.
3. Emotional reasoning.
4. Mistaking who you are today for who you will be tomorrow.
5. Believing that bigger is harder.
6. Failing to understand exponential growth.

Bias #1—Sunk cost fallacy: is the tendency to keep doing something because you've already invested a lot of time and effort into it. For instance, it is:

- Staying in the same relationship you've been in for years even though it's toxic.
- Pouring more money into your new venture because you've already invested so much into it.
- Keeping the same job because you've been there for years even though you hate it.

The truth is, the past is the past. If you've been spending the last ten years in a relationship that you shouldn't have gotten into, running a business you're sick of or staying at a job you hate, you should probably stop doing that. While your past doesn't determine your future, if you keep living in a past that you should have abandoned a long time ago, it certainly will. A powerful question to ask yourself if you want to overcome sunk cost fallacy is:

Knowing what I now know, if I were to start over today, would I still choose to do so?

- Knowing what I now know, would I still start that relationship?
- Knowing what I now know, would I still launch that new venture?
- Knowing what I now know, would I still stay at that job?

Usually, the answers are self-evident. You often know what to do but can't force yourself to do it. Remember, when you keep living in a present that should have become your past, you waste a tremendous amount of energy that you could be using to build the future you desire.

Now, we all fall for the sunk cost fallacy. Being aware of it doesn't immunize us against it, but it is the first step to avoiding falling for it.

Bias #2—Correlation is not causation: is the tendency to assume that there is a causal relationship between two or more events just because they seem to be related.

Because ice cream sales are correlated to the number of people drowning at sea doesn't mean one causes the other. It's just probably that there are more people eating ice cream and going to the beach in the summer. Because the stock price of a company dropped by five percent doesn't mean its CEO's tweets caused it. Stock prices fluctuate every day without anyone knowing why.

The point is, we tend to think in terms of cause and effect while reality is much more complex and nuanced than that. Our brain simplifies reality to help us navigate the world and make decisions. We try to find specific causes to explain historical events, such as wars or revolutions, but we can never truly grasp the full complexity of the world.

Remember, correlation is not causation. Look beneath the surface to try to understand better how reality works.

Bias #3—Emotional reasoning: is the tendency to assume that you can't do something unless you feel like it. It's thinking that your emotions must dictate your life.

Your ability to remain optimistic despite multiple setbacks is critical. However, no matter how much control you have over your emotional state, there will be times when your emotions will play tricks on you. For instance, you might not:

- Feel like working on your goals on any given day,
- Feel confident enough to ask for a promotion at work, or
- Believe that a certain goal is possible for you.

Feelings are tricky. Emotions fluctuate, but you are more than your emotions. What you feel at any moment says nothing about your capabilities and the extent to which you can grow, learn, and transform your life. Because you don't feel like working at any given moment doesn't mean you can't. You can ask for a raise regardless of your level of confidence. And whether you feel like a certain goal is possible for you is irrelevant. With a strong enough reason, you can learn any skill you need to reach any goal you have. Remember, one key to achieving extraordinary success is your ability to do what you need to do whether you feel like it or not. You are not your feelings. Stop behaving as though you were. Act even when you don't feel like it and start becoming extraordinary.

What about you? In what way are you falling prey to emotional reasoning?

Bias #4—Mistaking who you are today for who you will be tomorrow: is the tendency to assume that your future self will be the same as your present self.

One of the biggest mistakes you can make is to extrapolate your present self into the future. When you do so, you underestimate your future self's abilities. The truth is that your future self can be totally different from your present self—you can become extraordinary. But for that to happen you must think bigger, believe, and do the work in the present—start *today*. So, stop living in the limitations of the present. Live in the possibilities of the future. You can't fully grasp what your future self is capable of becoming. You will only know that in hindsight. You will only be able to connect the dots retrospectively.

Bias #5—Believing bigger is harder: is the tendency to believe that doing bigger things will be significantly harder than it will actually be.

Stop idolizing people. Stop perceiving world-class athletes, movie stars, or celebrities as being different than you. As human beings, we have more or less the same brain. And we share the same fears, worries, and insecurities. The people you look up to are often no more extraordinary than you are (or could become). Remember, you will grow into whatever challenges are thrown your way. You will become as big as your vision. This is why you must pursue an exciting vision that forces you to grow and become more. You can *choose* to become extraordinary. And this starts by realizing that bigger isn't necessarily harder. Nothing is too big for your future self.

Bias #6—Failing to understand the power of exponential: is the inability to comprehend how much we can grow over time.

Extraordinary results are seldom linear. The most common pattern is having years of mediocre results—or absence of results—until a tipping point is reached. Then, suddenly, growth becomes exponential. People often become an "overnight" success (after years of hard work).

As humans, we think linearly. We tend to overestimate what we can achieve in a few months while underestimating what we can achieve in a decade. The moment you work toward your vision, you activate the power of compounding. The moment you choose to be extraordinary, you are. It's just that results will take time to appear. You must pay the price in advance, in full, and with no money- or time-back guarantee. At first, it will seem as though nothing is happening. However, as you relentlessly improve your skills and move toward your vision, you'll start noticing results, until one day, you'll look back and be absolutely amazed by what you've accomplished.

The bottom line is that success is never an isolated event. It's always the result of a process that started long before the world noticed. Therefore, never stop working on your goals. Stay consistent. Make progress *every single day*. Focus on the process, and trust that the power of exponential growth will propel you forward.

* * *

Action steps

Complete the corresponding exercises in your action guide.

3

PERSONAL GROWTH

> " The big challenge is to become all that you have the possibility of becoming. You cannot believe what it does to the human spirit to maximize your human potential and stretch yourself to the limit.
>
> — JIM ROHN, BUSINESS PHILOSOPHER.

Thinking big and accurately is one thing, acting on those thoughts is another. As human beings, we never lack capacity. Our potential is nearly limitless, but we must do the work to unlock it. *Personal development is the ultimate leverage because it enables us to uncover our exceptional abilities and do the things that we once thought impossible.* Extraordinary results require extraordinary personal growth. For instance, through personal development you can:

- Increase self-awareness so that you better understand your strengths and weaknesses,
- Clarify your vision so that you can take inspired actions toward your ideal future,
- Strengthen self-confidence so that you act confidently toward your goals,

- Build discipline so that you do what you need to do whether you feel like it or not,
- Cultivate grit so that you keep going despite setbacks, failures, and disappointments,
- Nurture courage so that you can push past fears,
- Acquire mental models so that you can make better decisions,
- Learn new skills so that you can reach your goals, and
- Better control your emotions so that you can stay positive for as long as you need to reach your goals.

I. How to leverage personal development

Personal development is a wide topic. In this section, we'll focus on a few key principles that will make the biggest difference in your life. To learn about specific topics in greater depth, you can refer to my Mastery Series.

Here, we'll cover the following subjects:

1. Strengthening your self-confidence.
2. Building iron-clad discipline.
3. Cultivating extraordinary grit.

Think of each of these abilities as being on a spectrum. The greater your level of self-confidence, discipline, and grit, the more you can impact the world around you. Your goal is to bring each of these skills to an adequate level. In other words, if you seek extraordinary results, you must build unbreakable self-confidence, develop iron-clad discipline, and cultivate unshakeable grit.

I) Strengthening self-confidence

One of the best definitions of self-esteem is from the author, Nathaniel Branden. In his book, *The 6 Pillars of Self-Esteem*, he says:

"Self-esteem is the reputation we acquire with ourselves."

What determines our level of self-esteem is what we do—and, often, what we do when nobody is watching.

Becoming extraordinary entails being honest with yourself and doing your best with what you have. When you give your best and get back up after each setback, you start to develop self-respect. You may wish you could slack off and feel great nonetheless, but this usually doesn't work. Remember, self-esteem is the reputation that you acquire with yourself. To build more self-confidence and develop healthier self-esteem, try the following:

- **Repeat Meta-Beliefs and other empowering beliefs daily.** When taking a shower, walking, or before going to bed, think of empowering beliefs that will help you build the life you desire.
- **Act accordingly.** Positive self-talk is powerful, but it must be backed up with concrete action. The more you act in line with your beliefs, the more you'll strengthen these beliefs.
- **Do what you're afraid of.** Leave your comfort zone. Challenge yourself. Face your fears. As you move toward discomfort, you'll build more confidence over time.
- **Build self-discipline.** Your ability to set daily tasks and goals, and complete them consistently, will boost your sense of self-esteem.
- **Practice self-compassion.** When things don't turn out exactly as planned, always be kind to yourself. Avoid beating yourself up. Instead, practice compassionate self-talk. Tell yourself things such as, "It's okay," "You're doing the best you can.", or, "You'll do better next time."

Note that being self-confident doesn't mean you never doubt yourself. Self-doubt is a normal part of being human. Just don't let it stop you. Be self-compassionate. Always. Then, pick yourself up and keep going.

2) Building discipline

To achieve extraordinary results, you must do things you don't want to do, and this requires extraordinary self-discipline. Here is my favorite definition of self-discipline:

"Self-discipline is the ability to make yourself do what you should do when you should do it, whether you feel like it or not,"—Elbert Hubbard, writer and philosopher.

Self-discipline is another way to increase the reputation you have with yourself and build self-respect. It entails:

- Keeping promises to yourself, and
- Keeping promises to others.

A. Keeping promises to yourself

Do you often tell yourself you'll do something, but fail to do it?

When you keep breaking promises to yourself, it erodes your self-esteem. Imagine if every time you arranged to meet a friend, they didn't show up. Would you trust them? Would someone so unreliable be your go-to person whenever you faced major issues or needed help to complete an important task? This is the type of reputation you acquire with yourself when you fail to keep your word.

B. Keeping promises to others

Do you make empty promises? Do you overpromise and underdeliver? Do you say yes too often, but fail to follow through?

When you fail to keep your promises to others, you not only let them down, but you also let yourself down. And you know it. As a result, your words lose power. People stop listening to you. They cease looking up to you. They lose respect for you.

Here is the truth: you cannot achieve extraordinary results and impact the world at scale without help. You cannot rally others to your extraordinary vision if they don't trust you, and they will never trust you if you keep breaking your promises. Therefore, your goal should be to build your self-discipline to the point where you keep as many of your promises as possible.

Below are a few things that you can do to become more reliable:

Set small tasks each day and complete them. Building rock-solid self-discipline doesn't require doing anything extraordinary. Each morning, write down one or two simple tasks. Then, complete them without fail for thirty days in a row. Once you've reached thirty days, continue the challenge for ninety days, six months, and then one full year. Completing one or two tasks every single day for a full year will enable you to build momentum and dramatically increase your reliability and your self-confidence.

Make fewer promises. It's better to make fewer promises and keep them all than to make many promises and only keep eighty percent of them. People will respect you for setting boundaries and saying no, but they will resent you for breaking your promises. Therefore, make your "yeses" count. Give them power by becoming the most reliable person they've ever met. This way, over time, you'll build enough confidence to do extraordinary things.

Set bigger goals. As your self-discipline and confidence increase, you'll be able to set bigger and bigger goals.

Follow these simple tips and your confidence will inevitably grow over time.

3) Cultivating extraordinary grit

Most people say that they have big dreams. Yet, they tend to give up as soon as they face setbacks. Extraordinary people have unbreakable determination and unshakeable convictions. If you say that you want to make a difference, mean it. Pay the price. Fail over and over but keep going anyway. Use each setback as an opportunity to strengthen your mind and to recommit to your vision. Ordinary people who have become extraordinary all decided to continue no matter how many times they fell short of their aspirations. By doing so, they became high performers, often achieving more than they believed possible.

In many aspects, grit is what differentiates the ordinary from the extraordinary. And grit is learnable. You *can* build unbreakable grit.

Let me share a few things that you can do to develop more grit and determination.

A. Expect failures and prepare for the worst

You'll fail more times than you can imagine. Stuff will happen. Things outside your control will derail you from your path. You'll be disappointed, frustrated and even feel hopeless, at times. However, this is part of the process. Expect failures and prepare for the worst by doing the following:

- Acknowledge the fact that you will face many hardships along the way. Prepare to fail ten times more than you imagine. Then, see yourself getting back up over and over. It will train you not to give up when you face the inevitable challenges.
- Visualize yourself going through hell (the worst-case scenarios) and surviving and even thriving. See yourself being in the starkest moments as vividly as you can. Sense how you would feel in these circumstances. Then, decide that if such a situation happened, you would keep going. This will help you build the identity of someone who never quits.

The truth is, you cannot yet know the amount of grit required to reach your goals. The bigger the vision, the more determination you'll need. As you keep moving forward, you'll find out that you are far more resilient than you first thought.

B. Understand that when you feel like giving up it means the game is on.

Many people assume that, because they feel like giving up, they should. This is an example of emotional reasoning—i.e., believing that how you feel must dictate how you act. Fortunately, you don't have to become a slave to your emotions. I felt like giving up many times for many of my goals, in many areas of my life. I felt like giving up on writing. I felt like giving up on relationships. And I almost gave up on trying to have a meaningful career too.

But I didn't.

Ordinary people give up when they believe they can't take the pressure anymore. Extraordinary people never give up, knowing that they will eventually reach a breakthrough and become successful. When most people give up is the point when you must press forward. It's the point when you separate yourself from the crowd. It's the point when you move away from ordinary and turn toward the extraordinary. So, try one more time. Then, one more time again. And again. As the Japanese proverb says, "Fall seven times and stand up eight."

Always, always, always get back up and carry on.

C. Build the identity of someone who never quits

Many people give up too easily because they don't see grit as a value worth embodying. Quitting is merely something they do—another activity. But, as they keep abandoning their goals, quitting becomes part of their identity. In other words, quitting becomes who they are.

Extraordinary people see grit as a statement they make to themselves and to the world. They perceive themselves as being someone who never quits, and they seize every chance to embody this identity. Every opportunity to quit becomes an invitation to strengthen their determination and cultivate the identity of someone who refuses to give up.

Make quitting unacceptable. See yourself as having unlimited grit. You're just not the type of person who ever, ever quits.

D. See failure as a test from the universe

Setbacks, failures, obstacles, and disappointments are nothing more than tests. If your "why" is compelling enough and your determination strong enough, you'll pass the test. The world is merely asking you: "How badly do you want it?" When you keep going while having countless reasons to quit, you open yourself up to new opportunities. And, more importantly, you build your character and become the type of person who achieves the impossible. So, strengthen your desire and persevere until you pass the test—until you succeed.

E. Focus on the process

Many people are obsessed with results, but we cannot fully control the outcome. All we can do is focus on the process. To ensure you have the right process, ask yourself the following question:

"What could I do every day to almost guarantee that I will eventually achieve my desired outcome?"

Never underestimate the power of process. Daily actions performed consistently activate the power of compounding and, ultimately, lead to extraordinary results.

F. Reframe failure

We've been taught to perceive failure as something to avoid. This is the wrong way to see it. "Failure" is a man-made concept. The concept of "failure" creates a false dichotomy with failure on one side and success on the other. This is *not* how reality works. Success and failure are integral parts of the same process. Success is a trial-and-error process. It requires constant adjustments along the way. An airplane must constantly adjust its trajectory to reach its destination. Now, is an airplane failing every time it deviates from its trajectory? In the same way, we must continually adjust our actions in order to reach our goals. This is not failure; it is an integral part of the process we call success.

As the entrepreneur, Tom Bilyeu puts it, *"Failure is the most data-rich stream of information."* The more you take action and "fail," the more feedback you will receive, and the more you can refine your model of reality. Therefore, fail faster so that you can gather a larger amount of data. Then, get back up and keep going. Remember, you're simply not the type of person who ever quits. Use these techniques, and over time you'll become one of the most resilient people you've ever met.

In conclusion, to increase your impact, you need to develop extraordinary levels of confidence, discipline, and grit. And don't forget to stay consistent and remain patient. You are a lifelong project, and you are well worth the investment.

* * *

Action steps

Complete the corresponding exercises in your action guide.

4

TECHNOLOGY

> Attempting to succeed without embracing the tools immediately available for your success is no less absurd than trying to row a boat by drawing only your hands through the water or trying to unscrew a screw using nothing more than your fingernail.
>
> — RICHIE NORTON, ENTREPRENEUR AND AUTHOR.

Another powerful form of leverage is technology. *Technology enables you to gather more energy by using new tools that can replace human labor or do things that no human can do.*

For instance, the internet enables us to share content with millions of people all around the world instantaneously. Now, if we had to do that using human labor, it would require an enormous amount of time and effort and the work of countless people. To increase your available energy and make your vision a reality, you must use technology. Some examples would be:

- Using social media sites to expand your reach and increase your impact.

- Utilizing automation tools to schedule your content or send automated emails to your customers.
- Leveraging AI software to help you with your work whether you're a programmer, a writer, or an entrepreneur.

I. How to use technology to scale your impact

There are mainly two ways to boost your productivity and increase your impact by using technology. The first is to put in place automation and processes. The second is to leverage the power of algorithms. Let's have a brief look at each.

1)Automation and processes

Nowadays, we have access to thousands of apps. By using them effectively, we can free more of our time and use it to do what's most important to us.

For example, my assistant creates my social media posts and schedules them using a piece of software. By doing so, I'm using two forms of leverage. First, I'm leveraging other people's energy—i.e., my assistant's time. Second, my assistant uses technology to schedule the posts. As a result, I have more time available to work on high-value tasks—such as writing this book.

Here is another personal example. I've created templates detailing each step that goes into self-publishing and marketing a book. To do so, I used Google sheets (technology) and QuickTime player (technology) to create videos for each step. Then, I asked my assistant to follow the process whenever we publish a new book (other people's energy).

The point is, to enhance your impact, you must use technology. By leveraging technology, you'll be able to scale and/or free your time so that you can have a more balanced life. Sadly, many people work way too hard for way too little reward. That's often because they fail to use technology to increase their impact and multiply their time. If you don't clone yourself to magnify your impact, you'll end up doing the work of several people, and you will risk burning out.

2) Algorithms

In today's age, algorithms play a major role in our lives. They determine the content we see online, confirming our current beliefs instead of opening us up to new ideas. They also force creators to generate more content to feed the beast, sometimes leading them to exhaustion. In some respects, we've become slaves to algorithms. However, algorithms can also work in our favor, enabling us to multiply our impact by many orders of magnitude. Below are some ways to make the most of the algorithms.

- **Imitate successful people.** Study them carefully and try to identify what works and what doesn't. When possible, buy courses from successful content creators.
- **Keep experimenting until you find what works.** Often, our initial strategy or idea won't work. Keep testing your processes. "Throw spaghetti at the wall and see what sticks." Of course, avoid doing so randomly. Use what you've learned from successful people and make your best guesses. Then experiment.
- **Have a long-term vision.** Don't expect immediate results. From the beginning, give yourself time to figure things out. It can often take months or years before you notice significant results.
- **Stay consistent.** Once you've found what works, don't jump from one strategy to the next. Focus on the process. Do what you have to do each day until you achieve tangible results.
- **Focus on one thing at a time.** Focus on mastering one algorithm before moving on to the next platform (unless you have a team and can delegate the work). For instance, if you use ads to sell your products or services, don't run Facebook, Amazon, Google, Pinterest, and TikTok ads at the same time. Focus on one platform. Mastering just one ad platform at a time will be far more effective than dabbling with five.
- **Look out for new trending platforms.** Observe what trends are emerging. Then, experiment with new platforms. They can often give you more visibility and the competition won't

be as fierce. But before investing a lot of your time and effort, I suggest that you wait for a year or two to see if the platform will stick around.

- **Make sure you have a clear message/branding.** When you speak with your friends, you can afford to talk fast, be somewhat incoherent, and still get your point across. However, when you speak to millions, your message must be crystal clear, simple, and straight-to-the-point.

Keep in mind the points above as you work to improve your visibility online. Then, work on "breaking" the algorithm and see your impact explode.

To sum up, technology is a powerful form of leverage that, when used wisely, can enable you to skyrocket your results and magnify your impact. Technology allows you to capture people's attention at scale and direct it toward your mission. Attention is focused energy. And gathering the focused energy of millions of people is one of the most effective ways to scale your impact. Whoever can capture attention at a massive scale can transform the world.

Use technology to increase your impact. To enhance your impact, you must capture the attention of the world and direct it toward your inspiring vision.

* * *

Action steps

Complete the corresponding exercises in your action guide.

5

FOCUS

 If you do one thing and you do it right, and you do it all
the way, you can get as big as you want.

— ALEX HORMOZI, ENTREPRENEUR.

As the saying goes, "You can do anything, but not everything." The
biggest dilemma we face as human beings who want to succeed is
that we have limited time but almost unlimited potential. As a result,
to live a meaningful life we must choose what to do with our time
carefully.

Put simply, *focus is the ability to gather our energy and direct it toward a*
specific goal for long enough to make it a reality. Most people are unable
to use the power of focus effectively. By overestimating what they can
do in the short term and underestimating what they can do in the
long term, they never tap into the incredible power of focus. In other
words, these people fail to channel their limited energy and
compound it over time.

The point is, you can't achieve tangible results unless you channel
your energy effectively. This is why focus is one of the most powerful
tools you have. Use it appropriately and see your results explode. Fail

to leverage it and pay the consequences. Remember, when you lack focus and direction, you leak your precious energy every day—energy you will *never* get back.

1. How to leverage focus

If what you do today isn't moving you closer to where you want to be in ten years—then, it's keeping you away from it. Most people spend most of their time doing things that have no long-term impact. They spend hours watching TikTok videos, looking at Instagram pictures, or scrolling through their Facebook newsfeed. None of these activities will matter tomorrow, let alone ten years from now.

To impact the world at scale, you must align your daily actions with your long-term vision. The level of impact of an action is largely proportional to the scale and timeframe of your vision. An action that is part of a twenty-year vision is infinitely more powerful than an action that is totally random. That's why having a clear, compelling vision is so important and so powerful. It enables you to channel your energy and ensure that each of your actions has impact. As you take impactful actions one after the other, consistently, day after day, you will inevitably end up having a bigger influence over the world.

In other words, one key difference between an extraordinary person and an ordinary one is that the extraordinary person has a bigger and clearer vision and, as a result, takes more impactful actions, more often.

Now, let's review the three types of focus and see how you can use each to develop laser-sharp focus.

1) The 3 types of focus

Roughly speaking, we can identify three types of focus:

- Short-term focus (concentration),
- Transitional focus (planning/routine), and
- Long-term focus (vision).

Once you become an expert at utilizing them, your ability to focus will dramatically increase. Let's briefly look at each in turn.

A. Short-term focus (concentration)

Your ability to focus deeply on the task in front of you is one of the most powerful skills you can develop. That is truer in today's world where distractions are everywhere. Focus is raw energy. The more you channel your energy toward the vision you want to reach and the person you want to be, the more powerful you become. Conversely, the more you leak energy by jumping from one task to the next, checking your phone, or multitasking, the *less* powerful you become. Therefore, make it a priority to eliminate any distractions and focus on your most important tasks.

How to eliminate distractions

We can differentiate between two types of distractions.

1. Internal distractions, and
2. External distractions.

Internal distractions occur when your mind tries to interrupt you from doing important work. For instance, it may manifest as a sudden urge to go for a walk, grab a coffee, or check your emails. It may also be disguised as a thought that you need to complete a certain chore first. All of these are your mind's attempts at seducing you into doing what's easy instead of what's necessary.

External distractions are everything in your direct environment that has the ability to disturb you while you're working. For instance, it could be a colleague interrupting you, some noise distracting you, or notifications popping up on your phone or laptop.

Let's see what you can do to deal with both types of distractions.

1. Internal distractions

Your mind will often give you reasons to do everything but your important work. As you tackle your task, it will tell you that it's not good enough, that you can't do it or that you should take a break. It will create within you the sudden urge to work on an easier task or to message a friend. Whatever tricks it has up its sleeve, rest assured, it will try them on you.

The first step is to realize that this is normal. The more you understand how your mind works, the easier you will find it to design workarounds. The next time you work on an important task, notice what's going on in your mind. If you feel resistance, take note. Observe the content of your inner dialogue—the story you're telling yourself. As you do so, patterns will begin to emerge. Perhaps you feel the need to check social media. Perhaps you notice an urge to grab your phone. Or perhaps you feel like putting on music and dancing.

The second step is to put yourself in the right headspace. Many of us are chronically overstimulated. As we wake up, the first thing we do is grab our phone, read emails, or go on social media. In short, we're always on the lookout for external stimulation that will spice up our daily life—or so we hope.

All of these activities put us in a state of overstimulation and can make us feel restless. Not surprisingly, when it comes time to concentrate on important work that requires our undivided attention, we can't. Our mind is showing resistance. We're not giving it enough of the stimulation it craves. The solution is to eliminate distractions and keep your mind quieter. It will make it far easier for you to focus on your work. More specifically when you wake up avoid:

- Checking your phone,
- Turning the TV on, and
- Accessing the internet.

In addition, turn off all notifications on your phone (put it on airplane mode if you can). Then, keep your mind relaxed. For instance, you can:

- Meditate for a few minutes,
- Do some stretching, and/or
- Listen to relaxing music.

If you make it a habit to do these things each day, you'll see incredible results. For more on eliminating internal distractions, you can refer to my book, *Dopamine Detox*. Now, to reduce internal distractions even further, you can try the following:

- **Keep a to-do list.** Doing a brain dump and writing all the things you need to do today or in the near future further helps appease your mind. You're telling your mind that you know what you have to do.
- **Add items to your to-do list when needed.** Every time you remember something you need to do or feel the urge to focus on anything but the task at hand, add the item to your list. Then go back to work.

2. External distractions

External distractions are external stimuli that make it harder for you to focus. In most cases, they are interruptions. For instance, it may be someone calling you on the phone, your boss asking you to complete an assignment, or your colleague chatting with you. To build extraordinary focus, remove as many external distractions as you can. To do so, isolate yourself, which might entail:

- Wearing noise-canceling headphones.
- Asking your colleagues not to disturb you during specific hours.
- Telling people that you need to complete a key task right now and you will contact them later.
- Blocking time to work on your most important tasks.
- Waking up earlier to tackle your key task (for instance, if you're working from home with a spouse and kids, or in an office with a demanding boss or chatty coworkers).

The point is this. Ordinary focus cannot lead to extraordinary results. You must develop the ability to focus on the task at hand and eliminate any distractions (internal or external) that could prevent you from doing your best work. If you're reading this book, it means that you want to make a big impact. It also means the work you do each day matters—a lot. Treat it as such. Reclaim your focus.

B. Transitional focus (planning/routine)

Our mind always looks for opportunities to take it easy. Whenever you're unsure what to work on, your mind will seduce you into relaxing or filling time by working on unimportant tasks. This is why you must implement a system that enables you to switch from one task to the next smoothly. I call it "transitional focus."

How to build transitional focus

Disorganized people jump from one task to the next during the day. They neglect the big picture. They forget which tasks truly matter and why. In doing so, they lose the sense of priority, and they end up wasting time.

Don't be like them.

To increase your transitional focus, plan effectively and put routines in place. By planning your day, you know exactly what you have to do and in what order. As a result, your mind will have a harder time distracting you. The point of planning your day and creating routines is to channel your energy instead of having it leak away all day long.

How to plan your day

Planning is channeling your energy toward the activities that matter the most. Planning ensures that you spend most of your time on important tasks. When you plan your day each morning (or the evening before) you build momentum. And as you tackle your most important task(s) every day, you activate the power of compounding. This is the most effective way to focus your energy on achieving extraordinary results.

By writing down key activities, you can organize your mind better. Doing so also reduces the tendency for your mind to distract you. In a way, you're telling your mind, "I know what I have to do today, so you don't need to help me figure out that part." Below is a simple, yet powerful, method to organize your day.

Step #1—Identify your one key task

Ask yourself the following questions:

- If I could only work on one thing today, what single task or action would have the biggest impact (i.e., move me closer to my goal or vision)?
- If I were to complete one task first, which one would make me feel good and enable me to create incredible momentum that would carry me throughout the day? (This is often the same task as above.)
- Which is the most mentally and/or physically taxing task that I have to complete today? What task do I want to do the least? (This can also be the same task.)

The most important task is often the one that you want to do the least. For instance, for a salesman, it might be calling prospects. For a speaker, it might be rehearsing their speech, and for a musician, it might be playing difficult musical pieces.

The truth is, we usually know what we should be doing—but we tend to procrastinate. We spend hours designing a logo instead of calling prospects. We read books like this one, instead of doing the work needed to reach our goals. Or we talk about our exciting projects, instead of keeping quiet and doing the actual work.

Step #2—Repeat the process with other key tasks

Once you've identified your most important task, repeat the process until you come up with a few more. Remember, it's not about doing more things, it's about doing more of what truly matters. Or, as Gary Keller wrote in *The One Thing*, "*You need to do fewer things for more effect, instead of doing more things with side effects.*"

Forget about "working hard." The universe doesn't care about how hard you supposedly work. It will only reward you when you "do the hard work." By "working hard," I mean doing a lot of stuff without a sound strategy or clear priorities. And by "doing the hard work" I mean, doing the actual work that will get you the extraordinary results you want.

The problem with working hard is that it doesn't require any strategy or vision. Nor does it require you to think hard. It's probably not asking for your undivided focus either.

On the contrary, doing the hard work, requires you to:

- Follow a clear strategy,
- Focus deeply, and
- Build the mental fortitude and discipline to do what's hard even when you don't feel like it.

Therefore, don't merely work hard, "do the hard work." Train yourself to do what's difficult and important rather than what's easy and unimportant. It's your ability to do the hard work, not to work hard that, in the long term, makes the difference between good results and extraordinary ones.

What about you? What would moving from working hard to doing the hard work look like for you?

Step #3—Work on your most important tasks

Now that you've come up with your key tasks, get started. Tackle your single most important task. Set a specific outcome or target, such as a number to hit or a set duration to allocate to your task. For instance, it could be a certain number of calls to make or words to learn in a foreign language. Or it could be setting aside an hour to make phone calls or planning the next task. When you've completed your task, move to the next one on your list. You may take a short break but avoid distractions. Don't check your phone, go on social media, or watch videos. Maintain your focus.

C. Long-term focus (vision)

Having a long-term vision enables people to increase their impact exponentially. Sadly, most people lack vision. They hustle, trying to tick off as many items as possible from their list, irrespective of their relevance. When they manage to complete enough tasks, they feel good. When they fail, they feel bad. In short, they work hard instead of doing the hard work.

Developing a long-term vision helps you focus on the bigger picture of your life. It enables you to take a bird's-eye view and craft a sound strategy that will lead to an extraordinary future. As a rule of thumb, the longer your time horizon is, the more impact your work will have. Conversely, the more short-term oriented your thinking is, the less potent your actions will be.

Thinking long term and working toward your vision consistently is the equivalent of gaining an extra twenty IQ points. You might think I'm exaggerating, but what do you think happens when what you do every day moves you a little closer to your ten- or twenty-year vision?

When you align most of your daily actions with your long-term vision, the following things happen:

1. **Each of your actions becomes far more impactful.** Because your present actions are connected to your future vision, your energy is channeled effectively, which creates tangible results over the long term.
2. **You build enormous momentum.** By making daily progress toward your vision, you generate momentum. In addition, your subconscious works on your vision 24/7, enabling you to come up with better ideas and new opportunities.
3. **You make time an asset, not a liability.** When you lack clarity, your time becomes a liability. Having a clear vision enables you to turn your time into an asset instead. With a clear path ahead, you will take consistent steps that compound over time. You accumulate more energy, stronger beliefs, better thinking, a higher level of self-discipline, more financial resources, and a bigger network. With more energy, you can scale your impact by many orders of magnitude.

The bottom line is this. Long-term focus is one of the best predictors of success. By keeping an eye on your long-term vision and moving toward it daily, you'll attain far better results. It's the inevitable outcome of channeling your energy toward a clear and compelling future.

Creating a long-term vision

Having a multi-decade horizon eliminates noise and forces you to focus on the few things that matter. It reduces distractions and turns your attention away from worries—and toward the future you wish to create. It also requires you to use one of the most powerful tools you have: your imagination.

I encourage you to create a thirty-year vision. Such a long-term vision compels you to focus on the contribution you want to make to the world, and on the best ways to express your talents, skills, and personality. And it demands that you answer the hardest questions in life such as the ones below.

- **Do I want kids?** Why and why not? If I do want kids, what do I need to do to raise healthy kids who, in turn, will raise healthy kids of their own? And, perhaps more importantly, who do I need to become? What past traumas do I need to address? What shortcomings do I need to overcome? What can I do to become a better role model for my family?
- **What meaning do I want to give to my brief passage on earth?** What does expressing my talents, gifts, and personality look like? What is the unique way I contribute to the world? What do I want to do to leave the world a little bit better? And again, who do I need to become to make all these things possible? What self-imposed limitations and social conditioning do I need to overcome?

Take plenty of time to think about your vision. Then, continuously rework it. See your vision as a blank canvas that you slowly turn into a masterpiece through countless revisions, profound introspection, and vivid imagination. The simple process of writing down your long-term vision, no matter how fuzzy it might be, will help you learn more about yourself and will be highly beneficial.

Now, let's see how to gain more clarity regarding your vision.

Craft your long-term vision

It's impossible to think long term unless you spend time envisioning your future. In other words, you need to have clarity regarding the ideal future you desire to create. Below are some questions you should consider:

- How do I want to impact the world?
- What strategy do I need to put in place?
- What specific skills do I need to learn?
- What character traits do I need to develop?
- Who do I need to surround myself with?

Carve out time to clarify your vision. The more intentional you are, the better results you will obtain. To help craft your vision, do the following things:

1. Think of the ideal future you want to create, and
2. Identify gaps you need to fill in order to move toward that ideal future.

1. Think of your ideal future

Take a pen and piece of paper and write down any ideas or visions you have regarding your ideal future. What do you want to do? What kind of person do you want to become? If you could accomplish the extraordinary, what would make you feel most proud?

For a moment, let go of any fear or limitations. Forget about being realistic. The point of your vision is to inspire you to become someone you're not yet, someone who is better, smarter, wiser, and more experienced than you are now. Your future self will inevitably be better than you are today. So, stop thinking from the reality you're currently in. Instead, start thinking from the future reality you *want* to live in.

2. Identify gaps

Right now, there is a gap between who you are and who you need to become. This is completely normal. Your goals should be transformative. That's the whole point of setting ambitious goals. To move closer to your vision, you will need to fill in the gaps in terms of:

- Skills,
- Character traits,
- Network, and
- Resources/people.

Let's go over each of these points briefly.

Skills

Any long-term vision will require that you to learn many skills. Below are some skills that you'll likely need to learn if you want to make a big impact on the world:

- **Communication skills (oral or written).** Your ability to communicate effectively both in speech and in writing will have a massive impact on the results you'll obtain (or fail to obtain). Successful people are outstanding communicators. Become one of them.
- **Leadership skills.** To impact the world, you must inspire people to change. The best way to become a leader is to lead yourself first. This entails being disciplined, displaying courage, having core values that you live by, and pursuing your goals relentlessly. Others must respect you before they can allow themselves to be inspired by you.
- **Marketing skills.** You can't have a big impact if nobody has ever heard of you, your products, your services, or your ideas. Now, marketing must start with your product. That is, your product must be so compelling that people can't stop talking about it. In a sense, your products, services, or ideas

are the marketing. Traditional marketing merely acts as an amplifier.

- **Sales skills.** We're all in the selling business. You'll need to sell yourself and your vision to the people around you. You'll need to become an effective salesman. One of the best ways to do that is by becoming the best version of yourself and living according to your deepest values.
- **Team building skills.** Nobody is self-made. We all rely on the support of countless others. You will need to surround yourself with skilled people so that you can scale and magnify your impact. Being passionate and having a clear compelling vision will help you attract the right people.
- **Critical/strategic thinking skills.** You must learn to think critically so that you can make better decisions and take more impactful actions. Without a great strategy, your impact will be limited. Hard work alone cannot make up for a poorly designed strategy—not when it comes to generating extraordinary results.

What about you? What skills do you need to develop to move you closer to your vision?

* * *

Action step

Take an inventory of the skills you need to develop using your action guide.

Character traits

You must become the type of person who can achieve your ambitious goals. To do so, you must develop character traits that you may not yet possess. As the late Jim Rohn said, "*The major reason for setting a goal is for what it makes of you to accomplish it.*" Below are some common character traits that you will most likely need to cultivate:

- **Self-discipline.** Self-discipline is the ability to make yourself do what you should do, when you should do it, whether you feel like it or not. No matter how driven you are, there will be times when you'll feel unmotivated. But a common trait shared by extraordinarily successful people is their ability to act regardless of how they feel. (For more on self-discipline refer to **Part II. 3. Personal Growth.**)
- **Resilience.** Winston Churchill said that *"Success is the ability to go from failure to failure without losing your enthusiasm."* You will inevitably encounter countless setbacks in all areas of your life. Your ability to learn from each of them, pick yourself up, and keep going is what will steer you away from a mediocre life and drive you toward an extraordinary one. (For more on resilience, refer to the following section: **Leverage #3—Personal Growth, 1. How to Leverage Personal Development, 3. Cultivating Extraordinary Grit.**)
- **Integrity.** Your values act like a compass. Your ability to identify the core values to live by will enable you to make better decisions faster. It will also help make you trustworthy and reliable. People will want to work with you, listen to you, and be led by you. Therefore, take time to define your values and live by them consistently. As the entrepreneur Alex Hormozi puts it, *"You only truly know the strength of your values when they are tested."* It's only when you have the ability to slack off that your work ethic is tested. It's only when you can steal without getting caught that your honesty is tested. And it's only when you have the opportunity to cheat on your spouse that your loyalty is tested.
- **Focus.** Your ability to achieve extraordinary results is closely linked to your capacity to focus deeply over the long term. World-class performers spend more time than most practicing their craft alone. You too must cultivate your ability to focus deeply. Focus enables you to direct your energy toward the task in front of you instead of dissipating it via mindless distractions and constant interruptions.
- **Emotional intelligence.** Your ability to understand others and work with them effectively is another character trait to

develop in order to magnify your impact. You cannot do everything alone. You must be able to inspire others and act in a way that leads them to respect you and want to work with you.

- **Humility.** You must be confident enough to make your goals come true, but humble enough to learn anything that is needed along the way. Ego is the enemy of learning, and lifelong learning is key to never-ending personal growth and extraordinary results. So, set aside your ego and learn as if your future depends on it—because it does.

What about you? What character traits do you need to develop to make your impossible vision possible?

* * *

Action step

Take the inventory of the character traits you need to build using your action guide.

Network

To achieve impossible things, you'll need a great deal of help. It doesn't matter who you know now. As you take action, over time, you'll create a network of people willing to support you. For now, think of all the people who could help make your impossible vision possible. Understand that your ability to attract talented people is directly linked to the clarity of your vision, the strength of your reason, and your track record of success. Don't beg people for help. Show them how committed you are through your actions and results.

Resources/People

Whenever you try to achieve something, ask yourself who could assist you. The questions below will help:

- Who has already achieved the goals I'm trying to achieve?

- Who possesses the character traits or skills I need to develop?
- What role models could be a great source of inspiration for me?
- What books, courses, seminars, mentors, or coaches could help me level up?
- Who around me might know the perfect resources I need to achieve my goal?

In today's Information Age, you can learn anything at an affordable price (and often for free). Therefore, no matter how ambitious your vision is, know and believe that you can acquire the skills needed to move you closer to it. Remember, you can learn everything that you need to help you succeed.

Live in your ideal future

Use every opportunity to inhabit the ideal future you wish to create. Marinate in your thoughts until they consume you and start creating your reality. Refine your vision over time. Write it down. Then read it every day. Make sure everything you do takes you a step closer to that vision, not away from it. Bear in mind that the intensity of your vision will only grow as strong as you visualize it, internalize it deeply, and cultivate a burning desire to achieve it.

To sum up, long-term thinking is a habit. As with any habit, it must be practiced consistently until it becomes ingrained in your mind and begins to bear fruit. You *can* learn to become a long-term thinker, and when you do, everything will change for you. Remember, life is a marathon, not a sprint. So, start living in the ideal future that you wish to see and take the first step toward becoming extraordinary.

* * *

Action steps

Complete the corresponding exercises in your action guide.

6

OTHER PEOPLE'S TIME/ENERGY

 Leadership is unlocking people's potential to become better.

— BILL BRADLEY, POLITICIAN.

You cannot impact the world at scale just by yourself. You must leverage other people's time and energy. *Leveraging other people's time and energy entails working with freelancers, contractors, and/or building teams to increase the amount of energy available to move you closer to your vision.* In most cases, this entails creating an organization (whether it be a business or a foundation). Now, if you boil down a business or foundation to its essence, all you need to get started is:

- A great product, service, or message that people resonate with, and
- One source of traffic/marketing strategy to start scaling your impact.

However, most people tend to create many products and have multiple sources of traffic. Either that, or their message is too vague to appeal to enough people. Such a strategy (or lack thereof) inevitably weakens the intensity of their focus and often leads to failure or mediocre results. By doing so, they never reach the tipping point.

Reaching the tipping point

By focusing on too many things and/or lacking clarity, you will never accumulate the energy required to achieve outstanding results. The fact is, there is a cost of entry to extraordinary results. And you can only pay the cost by using one of your scarcest resources—your focus.

Yes, the price to pay is sustained focus over a long enough period of time. You *must* generate enough energy to reach the tipping point. Now, if you are fortunate enough to have enough money and experience, you can "outsource focus" by hiring competent people and scaling intelligently. The billionaire CEO, Richard Branson, supervises over 400 businesses. He does so by being a master of delegation and an expert at leverage. With tens of thousands of employees and lots of money, he has accumulated an incredible amount of energy.

Unfortunately, you might not yet have the resources needed to delegate part of your work and scale your impact. This is why you must narrow your focus. Then, over time, you need to identify your highest leverage tasks, focus on them, and delegate the rest.

How to use your energy and focus

Below is an effective process to build and scale your business, project, or mission.

1. Test,
2. Amplify what works,
3. Amplify even more,
4. Create processes,
5. Build teams/find top talent, and
6. Remove yourself.

Step #1—Test (Be a venture capitalist)

At first, you will need to test many things. By doing so, you will eventually find what works best for you. The key is to test as many things as possible while spending as little time and resources as you can. Furthermore, you should seek to minimize risk. At this formative stage, you're simply gathering information regarding what works and what doesn't.

One of my friends wanted to import specific stones from Mexico to France. He was confident there would be a market for them. As a result, he planned to spend $40,000 on inventory. I immediately advised him not to take so much risk. I suggested there were better ways to test the market than to buy $40,000 worth of inventory. For instance, he could:

- Import small items and try selling them. Doing so would cost him only a few hundred dollars.
- Try selling items using Facebook ads. He wouldn't even need an actual product to do that. He could just test if people would click on the buy button.
- Contact stores to see if they would be interested in such a product.

None of the strategies above required an upfront investment of $40,000. The point is, see yourself as a venture capitalist. Throw a little bit of time and money at projects, knowing that most of them won't work. And always limit your risk as much as possible.

Step #2—Amplify what works (Milk your cow)

Once you've identified a product, service, and/or marketing strategy that works, amplify it. Many people fail to scale what works. They stay in the test phase, looking for a new product to add to their portfolio. In other words, they forget to milk their cow, looking for another cow instead.

This is a huge mistake.

When I started writing and publishing books, I remained in the test phase for some time. First, following the advice of book marketing gurus, I tried many things. For example, I:

- Posted inspirational quotes on Facebook,
- Published articles on my blog,
- Wrote guest posts,
- Tweeted,
- Created online courses,
- Published books,
- Coached,
- Recorded YouTube videos, and
- Went on podcasts.

Eventually, I realized that writing books and promoting them on Amazon was what worked best for me. So, I focused on doing that. Over time, the sales of one of my books took off. So, I spent most of my effort marketing it. As a result, I was able to multiply sales by more than twentyfold. In hindsight, I probably didn't amplify enough!

Step #3—Amplifying more (Milk your cow harder)

People almost always fail to amplify enough of what works. This goes for the products they offer as well as for their strengths and abilities. They make the error of thinking that they've already scaled, and that they've exhausted the market. As a result, they diversify, creating too many products or trying too many things instead of staying focused on what works.

In fact, some of the most successful businesses have very few products.

- Tesla has two main car models, 3 and Y. It didn't try to create dozens of different vehicles like other constructors. It merely amplified what worked while making continuous changes via over-the-air updates and manufacturing improvements.
- Apple doesn't produce a new phone every year. It makes continuous improvements to a product that's already working, the iPhone. And it has been doing the same thing for the past fifteen years.
- The Coca-Cola Company has a variety of products in its portfolio, but it spends tons of money marketing Coca-Cola, their most popular product. More than a century after its creation, it's still striving to expand its global reach.

The entrepreneur, Alex Hormozi, has a great example on the danger of diversifying. One of his friends had over sixty businesses making around eight figures a year in total. So, he asked him, "If you could snap your finger and eliminate all businesses but one, how easy do you think it'd be to grow that business?" His friend replied, "Oh my god, it would be easy to grow that business to thirty or fifty million." After sitting with the question for an entire year, his friend started shutting down business after business after business.

The same goes for our strengths and abilities. What we excel at comes easy. As a result, we become complacent and start allocating our time to other activities. But, to do extraordinary things and impact the world at scale, you must magnify your talents. You can't afford to be great, or excellent, you *must* become extraordinary. Now, if you're unsure what your strengths are, here are a few things you can do:

- Take the StrengthsFinder test. This online paid test will enable you to identify your five signature strengths.
- Notice when people struggle to do things that seem so easy to you. You're probably on to something.

- Observe what people compliment you on. Is it your creativity? Your compassion? Your sense of detail? Your ability to speak in public?
- Ask your friends what your biggest strengths are.
- Take note of what you do in your free time. This shows you what you love to do, which is often linked to your strengths.

Once you have identified your talents, don't neglect them, and don't underutilize them. *Amplify* them. Spend a disproportionate amount of time polishing, nurturing, and refining them. Do whatever you can to keep improving. Assume there is always another level. Never think you're skilled enough. As the famous author, Stephen King, wrote, "*If God gives you something you can do, why in God's name wouldn't you do it?*" Your talents were given to you for a reason. Make the most of them and see what unfolds.

- If you're naturally compassionate, become even more compassionate. Aim at being the most compassionate person you've ever met.
- If you're naturally ambitious, embrace your ambition and use it to set a compelling vision that will lead to extraordinary results.
- If you're a natural leader, keep improving your leadership skills. Learn as much as you can on the topic and continuously ask for feedback.

Just a couple of talents or skills developed to the extreme can make all the difference to your ongoing success. They can transform you into a completely different person and enable you to do things you would never have imagined possible.

As for weaknesses, work on any skills that act as a bottleneck and can't be outsourced. In other words, if a skill is critical to the attainment of your vision, learn it no matter how many months or years it may take you, and learn it whether you feel like doing so or not.

The bottom line is, do not diversify too soon. Instead, amplify what works, then amplify it again and again. Do not underutilize your talents, amplify them—to the extreme.

What about you? Have you scaled your strengths or products/services to the extreme? Are you truly amplifying what's working for you? Are you nurturing your natural gifts and abilities? If not, you know what you have to do.

Step #4—Create processes

Once you've found a business, product, or idea that works, remove yourself. Do so by creating effective processes. These can be templates, checklists, standardization, or automation. The point isn't to remove yourself completely (unless you want to) but to free your time and mental energy so that you can focus on what you excel at, start new projects, or move to the next stage in your vision.

See processes as ways to channel your energy and the energy of others. Processes enable you to standardize your procedures, automate tasks, or hire and train people faster. McDonald's is an expert at standardizing their operations. Every step necessary to make a burger is written in detail. As a result, the company can hire people with little to no existing skills and train them quickly. To scale and make an impact, you must create outstanding processes in order to channel your energy and resources effectively.

Step #5—Build teams/find top talent

You don't have enough time and energy to acquire all the skills needed to scale your impact to the extreme. At some point, you'll have to surround yourself with people who already possess the skills you need.

Many people have a limited impact because they can never bring themselves to delegate their work. They become prey to their limiting thinking. It may be that they have no role models in their direct environment. Or they may fall prey to self-doubt, feelings of inadequacy, or limiting beliefs such as:

- I'm not the type of person who can... (manage a team, build a business, et cetera).
- I should be able to do everything myself.
- I'm self-made.
- I'm not good enough.
- I don't know how to do it.

As you gain access to more resources, especially money, you can scale even faster by working with talented people who can either:

- Make up for skills you lack, or
- Take off your hands the tasks that aren't the best use of your time.

Working with top talent frees up your time to work on high-leverage tasks and magnify your impact. People with world-class talent have years of experience. Because they know what works, they channel energy far more effectively than you ever could. As a result, they increase the total amount of energy you have to propel your vision forward. Unfortunately, people waste a great deal of time on tasks that they have no business engaging in. It might be fine for a majority of people, but it's unacceptable for anyone who wants to scale their impact exponentially. Now, why don't people work with top talent more regularly? Below are a few reasons:

- They are control freaks. They struggle to let go and entrust part of their work to someone else. They can't accept the idea that the people they work with won't always come up with the exact result that they had in mind.
- They have the wrong mindset. Instead of seeing delegation and outsourcing as an investment, they see it as an expense.
- They can't get past the initial investment required. They think it's easier to do it themselves than to outsource a task. That way, they won't need to find the right person, which takes time and effort.
- They prioritize their ego over the impact of their work. They may say they want to impact millions of people, but they

refuse to put in place the structure required to do so. Their behavior signals to the world that their ego and pride are more important than their lofty vision.

- They aren't ready yet. They're afraid of going to the next stage because it's new and uncomfortable.

The truth is, the most effective companies in the world have the most talented and smartest employees. You can't have extraordinary results by working with ordinary people. Yes, you can create an amazing culture and have a compelling vision that will inspire everyone to give their best, but you will still need to surround yourself with the most motivated and talented individuals you can find.

How to identify the right talent

There's no exact science to finding the right talent. However, here are a few things to consider:

- First, you must have a clear vision. This will enable you to take an inventory of the skills and resources required to move you toward it.
- Second, now that you know the skills you need, you must identify what skills you lack or need to delegate.
- Third, you must look for highly talented people who possess the exact skills you need. Start by asking your current network if they can recommend someone. If not, ask them if they know someone who could. Finally, do your own research. Look for people who have already achieved what you seek to achieve. You want them to have already done the things you want to do many times over.
- Fourth, write down your vision and broadcast it to the world. It might enable you to find highly motivated and talented people who are excited about your vision and want to join you on your journey.

Step #6—Remove yourself (Move on to a new venture)

The final step is to put in place processes that enable you to remove yourself if you choose to. You can stay in your business and use the time you freed up to focus on high-level strategies and key tasks to scale your impact further. Or you can move on to a new venture. Either way, you can repeat the process below:

1. Test,
2. Amplify what works,
3. Amplify even more,
4. Create processes,
5. Build teams/find top talent, and
6. Remove yourself.

This is what highly successful people do to scale. In the end, you're just one person. Unless you use all of the forms of leverage mentioned in this book, you won't be able to make a massive impact on the world around you.

* * *

Action steps

Complete the corresponding exercises in your action guide.

7

MONEY

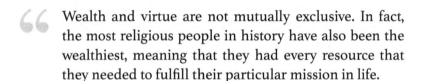 Wealth and virtue are not mutually exclusive. In fact, the most religious people in history have also been the wealthiest, meaning that they had every resource that they needed to fulfill their particular mission in life.

— GARRETT B. GUNDERSON, ENTREPRENEUR.

Money is many things to many people, but for people seeking to become extraordinary, it's an incredible tool that they can use to enhance their contribution to the world. Every influential person in history had to use money to amplify their reach and increase their impact. That goes for non-profit businesses like charities as well. The biggest charities in the world can raise millions of dollars to help solve issues they deem important. In other words, they are able to channel the stored energy (money) of many thousands of people to make a difference in the world.

Remember, the magnitude of your impact is determined by the amount of energy you accumulate using leverage. You must become a master at accumulating a massive amount of energy and channeling it effectively to move you toward your vision. Whether you think money is good or bad is irrelevant. *Money is simply a tool that enables you to scale your impact.* Money is stored energy, and you need all the energy you can generate.

Now, let's see how you can use money to increase your impact.

1. How to use money to scale your vision

Roughly speaking there are two different ways to use money to amplify your impact.

1. Investing in yourself, and
2. Investing in your business.

1) Investing in yourself

Your vision, business, charity work, or any other endeavor, is limited by your level of personal growth. When you see your venture stagnating, it is often a sign that *you* are stagnating. You haven't invested enough in yourself, and you haven't worked with coaches or mentors to break through mental barriers and limitations. The point is, in any of your ventures, you are always the limiting factor. You're the bottleneck. You're the problem, but you're also the solution. For example, the only reason I haven't yet multiplied my impact by a factor of ten is because:

- I haven't clarified my why and strengthened my desire enough.
- I haven't invested enough in myself and developed the skills required to scale my business.
- I didn't surround myself with enough top talents due to limitations and fear around building teams.
- I've been saving too much of my money instead of reinvesting it to grow my business.

To scale, you must use money to acquire the skills you need to reach your goals. Seek out the people who have already achieved the type of results you're looking for. Then, work with them. The more directly you can work with world-class people, the better. And the more money you have, the easier it will be to work one-on-one with them.

How to increase the ROI on your personal investment

You won't always know whether your investment will pay off, which is why you must adopt the mentality of a venture capitalist by running tests until you find what works. When you identify something interesting or helpful, lean into it. However, before investing in yourself, consider the following points:

1. **Level of impact of the skills.** Some skills have little impact while others make a huge difference. Ask yourself what skills do I need to invest in that will have the biggest impact on my personal and/or professional life?
2. **Level of alignment of the skills with your goals.** A skill can be useful to one person, but useless to another. It depends on how the skill fits into their vision. For example, if you want to become an outstanding writer, it doesn't make sense to learn how to program mobile apps. Similarly, if you aspire to be the next Lebron James, learning woodwork won't help.
3. **Level of enjoyment.** If there is something you enjoy, do more of it. It might stay just a hobby or develop into a career. Either way, investing time and effort in it might make sense. It will enable you to find more fulfillment or help you relax after a long day.

To accelerate your impact, use your money to learn valuable skills—communication skills, leadership skills, thinking skills, and learning skills. The long-term payoff will be massive. Find the best resources and invest money now. Learn more. Move faster. Scale further. And become extraordinary.

* * *

Action steps

- Find where you're lacking the skills needed to scale your impact. What's your limiting factor?
- Put an action plan in place to acquire those skills or to work with people who already have those skills.

2) Invest in your business

The second-best way to leverage your money is to invest in your business. Investing in your business can have a far higher return on investment than any other investment vehicle (stock market, rental properties, cryptocurrency trading, etcetera). Now, investing in your business might mean:

- **Investing more money into marketing.** Whenever I catch myself saying "I spent X amount of money this month on ads," I stop and rephrase it as follows, "I *invested* X amount of money this month on ads." Many people mistake investing for spending. Anything that enables you to grow yourself or your business is an investment, not an expense. When done effectively, marketing brings new customers that you can retarget later to offer them more products. Marketing also accelerates word of mouth and increases your visibility. As such, it's a great investment.
- **Taking courses or training to acquire practical skills.** You must learn new skills to grow your impact. Once you've identified the skills with the biggest leverage, find courses to help you learn them. Then, implement what you learn immediately. Whenever possible, invest in courses or training created by the most talented people in that specific field. It will save you a lot of time. And, by paying for them, you'll have more skin in the game and will be more incentivized to act.

- **Working with coaches or mentors.** Some experts have decades of experience in their field. Why not soak up their knowledge? For instance, I've started working with a coach to improve my American accent. I've been blown away by what I was able to learn. I spent the past decade trying to pronounce the "th" sound correctly. Yet, I've seen no improvement. But after my coach explained how the sounds were made, I learned to pronounce it in less than a minute.
- **Investing in your teams, business partners, and suppliers.** You want the people who work with you to grow. This is why you must invest in their professional and personal development as much as you can. For instance, buy them courses, training, or books. That goes for employees as well as contractors or freelancers. You want anyone who works with, or for, you to be motivated, to become better at their craft and to stick around.
- **Joining Mastermind groups.** Masterminds are small groups of motivated people. They meet regularly to brainstorm ideas, share their problems, and keep each other accountable. In Masterminds, you'll learn strategies and skills that can enable you to grow significantly. But this is not the most valuable part. The true purpose of Masterminds is to eliminate self-imposed limitations and discover what's truly possible for you. One of my friends joined a Facebook ads Mastermind. Before joining, he was spending $200 per day on ads and felt it was a stretch. Can you imagine his shock when, during the first call, one participant asked the organizer how to allocate his $300,000 monthly ads budget?

2. How to accumulate money

The more money you have, the more you can invest to grow your business. Now, the problem is that you don't always have the money needed at your disposal. This is especially true when you're starting out.

Fortunately, it doesn't have to be your money. You can leverage other people's money to grow your business and there are many ways to do so. Your ability to raise money is another powerful form of leverage. Put simply, raising money is borrowing the stored energy of other people instead of having to expend your own energy.

It's powerful.

Of course, borrowing money comes with many caveats and has its own set of challenges. But it's something to consider depending on your vision and how many resources you need to expend to move toward it. Don't forget that many investors are willing to put millions of dollars into dubious projects. The cryptocurrency mania we've seen recently is a perfect example of this phenomenon. We've seen one scam after another, one useless project after the next. On the other hand, with a solid enough project, you can find ways to raise money.

You can use other people's money in several ways, whether it is by running a crowd funding campaign, getting a loan, or raising money for your startup. The specifics of how to do this is beyond the scope of this book. I would just encourage you to apply what you've learned from this book—the Law of Beliefs, Meta-Beliefs, Mastery Mindset, et cetera—in order to find the information you need, and then execute it effectively to reach your goals. Remember, you can learn any skill you need to achieve any goal you have. And raising money is also a skill that you can learn.

3. Increasing the velocity of money

Money is energy. The more you can gather, the more things you can do—and the bigger the impact you can have. But it's only potential energy until it's put to use and circulated. Therefore, another key aspect to consider in order to increase your impact is the *velocity* of money. That is, how fast you can put your money to good use, earn it back, and reinvest it. In other words, how fast you can circulate it. The more often you reinvest the same dollars, the more energy you will generate.

For instance, let's say you invest $1,000 on ads each month and break even (i.e., get your $1,000 back). That's $12,000 invested each year. Now, imagine you invest $1,000 per day and also break even. Over twelve months you'll have invested $365,000, or thirty times more. On paper, it may look the same, but it has different implications. Investing thirty times more money means that:

- You can significantly increase your visibility. By spending thirty times more you'll be far more visible, creating bigger word of mouth. If your product, service, or mission is compelling, it will accelerate your growth.
- You can gather more data. The more action you take, the more feedback you gather. For instance, you may gain new insights on how to improve your products or services. Or you may be able to identify your ideal customer.
- You gain more customers. By spending more on ads, you'll make more sales, which means you'll have more customers who may buy more products later or recommend your products to their friends.

The example above might not be wholly realistic, but it illustrates the power of increasing the velocity of money. Money is stored energy. It doesn't do much unless you use it to accelerate your success. Money is here to help you grow and accelerate your impact. It's an accelerator, a powerful form of leverage.

Now, investing in ads is just one example. You can invest your money in any endeavor that will help scale your business faster. For instance, it could be working with a coach, hiring top talent, or making tests to find new ways to promote your products. The point is, increasing the velocity of money can enable you to grow faster because it activates the power of compounding.

The same concept can be applied to your personal life. Many people fail to invest enough in themselves. As a result, they stagnate. Accelerating the velocity of money in your personal life means continuously investing in invaluable resources that can generate a positive ROI. You won't always get it right. Sometimes, you'll buy a book, go to a seminar, or invest in a course that isn't useful. But more often than not, you'll benefit from your learning. So, increase the velocity of money to accelerate your growth.

* * *

Action steps

Complete the corresponding exercises in your action guide.

8

KNOWLEDGE

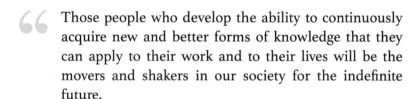 Those people who develop the ability to continuously acquire new and better forms of knowledge that they can apply to their work and to their lives will be the movers and shakers in our society for the indefinite future.

— BRIAN TRACY, MOTIVATIONAL SPEAKER AND
AUTHOR.

Today, we are living in an incredible world where knowledge is accessible to almost anyone. Knowledge is another powerful form of leverage you must use if you are to attain extraordinary results. Put simply, *leveraging knowledge means leveraging the collective time of the entire world population (past and present)*. If we had to reinvent the wheel every time we wanted to do something, we would waste most of our time building things that have already been built or solving problems that have already been solved. We do not have the luxury to do that.

Knowledge enables us to accelerate our results and multiply our impact. It saves us time. In a sense, knowledge, like money, is stored time. By tapping into collective knowledge, we accumulate more energy—the energy others have already invested to generate that knowledge. For instance, by reading books, you can soak up decades of accrued knowledge from experts in any field.

In this section, let's see how to use knowledge effectively so that you can increase the amount of energy you accumulate and move closer to your vision.

1. How to use knowledge effectively

It's often said that knowledge is power. However, in truth, knowledge is only *potential* power. To be of any use, knowledge must be activated and turned into experiences and inner wisdom.

Now, acquiring knowledge isn't just about reading books or listening to podcasts. Soaking up knowledge requires a specific mindset, which we'll explain in this section. When used intelligently, information enables you to learn faster and accumulate more energy in the form of practical knowledge. When used mindlessly, it destroys your focus and prevents you from reaching your goals.

1) The three stages of knowledge

Unfortunately, reading dozens of books doesn't guarantee that you'll acquire the skills you need to reach your goals. Many people overindulge in educational content. The more they "learn", the better they feel. They mistakenly believe that they are learning.

But are they?

Let's look at the results. Do they make more money? Do they have more fulfilling relationships? Do they feel better? Are they producing higher-quality work? Did they lose those extra pounds of bodyweight?

Results never lie, only people do.

Consuming information is useless unless it's followed by concrete action. For instance, "There is nothing new here", "I didn't learn anything," or "I already knew that," are often comments from people who lie to themselves. These individuals believe that they need to learn more while in reality, they need to *do* more. There is a huge difference between knowing something intellectually and having incorporated it in your life. It's the difference between obtaining mediocre results and extraordinary ones—it's what separates masters from amateurs.

The point of acquiring knowledge is to help effectively channel your thoughts and actions to move you toward the goal you desire. The value of knowledge is that it helps you use your energy more effectively so that it has more impact. This is why passively consuming books isn't particularly useful. To be beneficial, learning must lead to an actual reorganization of your thoughts and actions. Now, let me share with you the three stages of knowledge that I find useful.

1. **Knowing.** It's when you know something intellectually. For instance, you probably know that you should exercise more, stop eating so much junk food, or go to bed earlier.
2. **Doing.** It's when you actually *do* something with the information you consume. For instance, after reading this book, you may set bigger goals, exercise a little more, or reduce your intake of sugar.
3. **Living.** It's when you do something consistently until you turn intellectual knowledge into practical skills, and then develop deeper wisdom that leads to inner transformation.

Unfortunately, most people stay at stage 1 (knowing) or stage 2 (doing). That is:

- They consume educational content and feel good about it, but they don't do anything with the information (knowing). It remains useless knowledge that they have stored somewhere in their brain and may retrieve once in a while to look smart or impress people.
- They might read a book and feel inspired to take action (doing). They set new goals such as to eat healthier food or hit the gym. But, soon enough, the initial excitement wears

off and they give up. Later, they'll pick up yet another book or course and repeat the cycle all over again.

To achieve tangible results that will transform your life, you *must* move to stage three (living). This is where the magic happens. This is where you separate yourself from most people. Living means *embodying what you learn*. It's not merely knowing it intellectually. It's knowing *intuitively*. It's when you've integrated the lesson and made it part of who you are. For instance, it's when:

- You've been learning a new language daily for over five years.
- You've been painting daily for the past three years.
- You've been practicing martial arts three times a week for the last ten years.

The point is, you only truly know something once you've done it consistently. You need to practice it until it becomes a habit—part of your whole being. If you don't live it, you don't know it. You can think of this process as "transferring a skill from the conscious to the subconscious." At first, everything you learn requires your full attention. Your conscious mind must be in charge, which makes the process energy-draining. However, as you keep practicing, it becomes more and more automatic.

For instance:

- The first driving lesson is overwhelming, but, over time, driving becomes almost effortless.
- Learning to dance is awkward at first but, with enough practice, it becomes natural.
- Practicing a new language requires a great deal of mental effort. However, as you become better, it becomes easier.

If you're not getting results in your life, chances are that you're stuck in the "knowing" or "doing" phase. If this is the case with you, it's time for you to move to the "living" phase, which entails cultivating a mastery mindset.

2) Developing a mastery mindset

A mastery mindset is the fundamental mindset you must acquire to achieve any goal you desire. Once you understand it and embody it, it will completely transform your life. That's why I mention it over and over in my work. I want you to understand how powerful it is, not just by *knowing* about it—but by *living* it.

In this section, we will discuss in depth what the mastery mindset is and how you can cultivate it.

A. What is the mastery mindset

The mastery mindset is the realization, the inner belief that everything is learnable. It's the deep understanding that, if you stick to the process long enough, you can learn any skill that you need to reach any goal you set.

It's based on the following core principles:

- **Your mind is an unstoppable learning machine.** We all have similar brains. If someone else was able to acquire a skill or reach a specific goal, so can you. Your brain is a learning machine. You just have to tell it what you need to learn and get started.
- **You have far more grit than you believe.** Many people give up on their goals too easily. In truth, you have far more grit than you can imagine. As you keep going despite the inevitable setbacks, you will uncover deeper levels of tenacity within yourself.
- **The process is the key.** The results you obtain are always the direct consequence of a specific process. Consequently, focusing on the process is always more important (and more effective) than obsessing over the results.

You probably notice overlaps with the three Meta-Beliefs we discussed earlier. This is great. The more you internalize empowering beliefs from various angles and in various ways, the more tangible these beliefs will become. In fact, one key aspect of the mastery mindset is quite simply *repetition*. The truth is, you don't need to understand dozens of concepts to transform your life. You merely need to grasp a few concepts at an extraordinarily deep level.

B. The key aspects of the mastery mindset

Below are the main components of the mastery mindset. Someone who possesses a mastery mindset is:

A master of the process

Behind every success is a process. Mastering the process involves identifying the most effective ways to reach your goals, creating a method, and sticking to it until you attain your target. The process is all that matters; it's the only thing you ever have control over. When you do what you have to do every day, even when you don't feel like it, you will eventually become a master of the process and the shaper of your future success.

A master of implementation

Masters excel at transforming intellectual knowledge into concrete actions, and then, internalized wisdom. By taking action consistently, they receive invaluable feedback from reality. When they fail to get the results they want, they analyze their behavior, looking for the missing piece(s). They understand that the difference between success and failure is in the details. By tweaking, refining, and optimizing, they eventually find the missing piece(s) and achieve the outcome they desire.

A master of humility

Masters never blame the process or their circumstances when they fail. Instead, they question themselves and reassess the process. They aren't afraid of returning to the fundamentals to find out where they might have gotten things wrong. Whenever necessary, they swallow their pride and ask for help from anyone who may know the answers they're looking for. In short, masters always prioritize learning over ego and pride.

A master of repetition

Every master was once a disaster. Masters overcome their limitations through relentless repetition. Martial arts experts have practiced the same kicks and punches tens of thousands of times. Chess grandmasters have internalized tens of thousands of patterns. And world-class musicians have rehearsed the same pieces of music over and over. The daily repetition of fundamental skills over a long enough period of time makes ordinary people extraordinary.

A master of grit

Masters never stop until they achieve their goals. They understand that unshakeable grit is the key to achieving almost any goal they can envision. They know that if they keep going, stay focused on the process, and continually learn from their mistakes, they will find a path to success. By refusing to give up, they build the identity of someone who never quits.

A master of faith

Masters have faith in their process. Once they have done all the preliminary work to ensure their process is effective, they trust the process. They know that if they keep doing what they need to do every day consistently, they will inevitably reach the results they want.

A master of long-term thinking

Masters are long-term thinkers. They project themselves into their ideal future and return to the present with a clear plan. Then, they execute daily. They enjoy the process, knowing that they're becoming better every day. They shape their future one day at a time, one step at a time, one small win at a time, inexorably moving closer to the extraordinary future they desire.

C. Invert your learning/action ratio

Most people fail to achieve extraordinary results because they "learn" too much and "do" too little. Except for a minority of high achievers, people just don't take enough action to build the confidence and momentum necessary to reach their goals.

Now, here is what I mean by "learning":

consuming content passively—reading books, watching videos, or going to seminars—without doing anything with it to move you closer to your goals.

And here is what I mean by "doing":

doing something that enables you to make tangible progress toward your goals.

For instance, "doing" could be:

- Coaching people if you're a coach.
- Building a business and doing things that move the needle forward (instead of spending weeks designing a logo or tweaking your business card).
- Actively dating or doing activities that increase your likelihood to get dates (and not merely reading relationship books or watching videos).

Taking massive action will solve most of your problems in most areas of your life. Therefore, invert your learning-to-action ratio. Whenever you learn something, do so with the intention of using it immediately. Develop extreme speed of implementation. Reduce the time between the moment you learn something and the moment you use that knowledge.

As a rule of thumb, aim at spending eighty to ninety percent of your time taking action and ten to twenty percent learning. This ratio will vary from one person to the next, and from one task to the next, and it will evolve. For instance, if you've already spent way too much time "learning," dedicate a larger majority of your time to taking action.

Note that you can almost never take too much action. I've seldom seen people fail by doing too much, but I've seen many people fail by doing too little. To become extraordinary, invert your learning-to-action ratio. Take more action faster. Build incredible momentum. And begin to transform your life.

D. Acquiring meta-skills

Different skills have different levels of impact. Just mastering a few skills can enable you to scale your impact massively. I call these "meta-skills." The more proficient you become at these meta-skills, the more your leverage will increase, and the greater your impact will be. Below are some of the meta-skills you might want to focus on to increase your overall impact.

Communication skills. Your ability to communicate effectively, both while speaking and writing, is essential. You must communicate your message clearly so that people understand it. The more you write and speak intentionally, the better thinker you will become. As the psychologist, Jordan Peterson, said, *"Writing is a powerful tool for personal development because it allows you to create order out of chaos."* In short, writing requires you to think. And so does speaking. As the French writer, Anne-Thérèse de Marguenat de Courcelle, noted, *"The first rule for speaking well is to think well."* The converse is also true. The better you think, the better you'll tend to be at writing and speaking.

Leadership skills. You can't make a difference in the world without the help of others. You must be able to rally people to your cause. You must lead them. This entails building the following skills:

- **Self-leadership.** This is your level of personal development. The more disciplined, self-aware, and committed to your vision you are, the easier it will be to encourage people to follow you. Changing others is one of the hardest things to do, and it is largely out of your control. Changing yourself is difficult, but it is within your control. As you change, people around you will feel inspired to change too.
- **Delegation.** Being able to let go of control and letting others work autonomously is essential if you want to magnify your impact. Your role as a leader is to give people the "what" (where to go), then get out of their way and let them figure out the "how" (the way to get there).

- **Prioritization.** Massive impact requires crystal-clear focus. You're responsible for identifying what truly matters and ensuring that all the resources you have are channeled toward that endeavor.
- **Team building.** You must surround yourself with top talent who will embrace your vision. Then, you must communicate with them and lead them effectively to bring the best out of them.

Thinking skills. Thinking well is one of the most important skills you can develop as it impacts everything you do. It affects how you communicate with others, which in turn affects every decision you make. Accurate and effective thinking dictates the quality of your strategy and determines the magnitude of the results you obtain. More specifically, you need to develop the following skills:

- **Accurate thinking.** This means improving your ability to see reality for what it is so that you can develop better strategies.
- **Strategic thinking.** This means having a sound strategy so that you make good decisions. The better you become at thinking accurately—through self-reflection, careful observation, and experience—the better you'll be at crafting a sound strategy.
- **Decision making.** This means making good decisions so that you can achieve the results you desire. Having a sound strategy will help you do this.

* * *

Action steps

Complete the corresponding exercises in your action guide.

CONCLUSION

Impacting the world at scale is *difficult*—extremely difficult.

To do so you'll have to be patient and reinvent yourself over and over again. You'll have to remove layers of self-imposed limitations and social conditioning. But as you do so, you'll begin to do "impossible" things, transforming your relationship with yourself. In the process, you'll ask yourself:

"How much more can I do?"

"What's truly possible for me in this world?"

As you challenge your limitations one by one, you'll start removing the idea of who you're supposed to be, and you will discover who you truly are. Now, impacting the world at scale will inevitably take you years, if not decades. And you'll have to master every single form of leverage mentioned in this book. It's only by doing so that you'll gather sufficient energy to make a difference. That is:

You'll have to internalize Meta-Beliefs deeply, truly believing that everything is possible, that everything is learnable, and that, for any issue you face, *there is a solution.*

You'll have to sharpen your thinking and see reality for what it is, not what you want it to be.

You'll have to leverage technologies to multiply your time, make algorithms work for you and explode your visibility and impact.

You'll also have to make your personal growth an ultimate priority so that you can leverage your skills and talents to the extreme and contribute to the world at the highest level possible.

You'll need to develop laser-sharp focus over the long term to activate the power of compounding and magnify your impact.

You'll be required to collaborate with other people and rally them to your cause in order to increase the amount of energy you can channel toward your vision.

And you'll need to accumulate as much money (stored energy) as you can so that you can utilize it to accelerate your progress and multiply your overall impact.

Finally, you'll have to gather knowledge so that you possess the right information and strategies to grow your impact and move closer to your vision.

In short, you'll have to do whatever you can to accumulate as much energy as possible. Remember that everything is energy, and when you capture enough energy and channel it toward a specific endeavor, extraordinary things happen.

To conclude, let's face it. You'll fail many times. At times, you'll be disappointed, frustrated and angry. But don't worry, this is all part of the process. Turning the knowledge that you've gleaned from this book into actual experience will take years. In fact, there is no end to that process. Like you, I'm still on my journey toward uncovering what I'm truly capable of becoming. The only thing I know is that I have only explored a fraction of what's possible for me—and so have you.

Reread this book as often as needed. Treat it like a manual to becoming extraordinary. Remember, every master is a master of repetition. Every key concept must be dissected and studied many more times than we think in order for it to become internalized and produce results in the real world.

You always have a choice.

You can choose to stay ordinary, or you can commit to becoming extraordinary. There is no right or wrong answer—but you must decide one way or the other.

ACTION GUIDE

Doing the Impossible and Being Extraordinary

Self-assessment

On a scale from 1 to 10 (one being not all, 10 being absolutely), assess how extraordinary you are right now in each area below:

Career:

0   10

Character (self-discipline, kindness, etc.):

0   10

Finance:

0   10

Health:

0   10

Relationships:

0   10

Define what extraordinary means to you

What does being extraordinary mean to you personally? What does the extraordinary version of you look like? How do you feel? What do you do? What impossible things do you attempt?

For a moment, let go of limitations and fears and envision the ideal version of yourself. Remember, being extraordinary means impressing yourself, not others. Focus on yourself and what *you* really want.

My vision of being extraordinary:

_____

_____

_____

_____

_____

_____

_____

_____

Do "impossible" things

Write down below your own list of "impossible" things to strive for. Don't worry about how realistic those things are. Write down what inspires you and energizes you. What things could you do that would make you feel absolutely amazing?

My list of impossible things:

_____

_____

_____

_____

_____

_____

_____

_____

_____

Part I. Fundamental Assumptions and Models of Reality

1. Fundamental Assumptions about Human Beings

Remind yourself of the 8 fundamental assumptions below. The deeper you internalize them, the more impact you can have on the world.

1. Energy is the currency of the world.
2. We have far more potential than we can ever imagine.
3. Incentives rule the world.
4. Fear and love are the two fundamental forces that drive human behavior.
5. Most of us want to be part of something bigger than ourselves.
6. Most of us do not know what we want (and will follow people who do know what they want).
7. We all believe we are right.
8. We are always trying to convince others of something.

Now, knowing these 8 assumptions, write down at least one concrete action you could take to increase your potential impact on the world around you.

How I can make these assumptions work for me:

_____

_____

_____

_____

_____

2. The Power of Assumptions

Assumptions are statements you believe to be true. They directly impact the results you achieve in life and work as follows:

Assumptions —> beliefs system —> thoughts —> words —> actions —> results.

Assume everything is possible until you have proven with relentless action that it isn't. Now, complete the following exercises:

Write down the one belief that you think is limiting you the most in life

My biggest limiting belief:

_____

Write down three disempowering assumptions preventing you from achieving your goals (i.e., I'm not smart enough, there is too much competition, I don't know the right people, etc.)

My three disempowering assumptions:

1.

2.

3.

Alternatively, think of one major goal that you'd like to achieve but don't believe is possible for you. Then, write down all the reasons or excuses why you believe it can't be done.

My major goal:

_____

Reasons why I believe I can't reach that goal:

_____

_____

_____

_____

Finally, practice reminding yourself that everything is possible unless proven impossible. That is, assume you can, take action, and see what happens.

3. The Three Laws of Belief

The world obeys specific laws. When you fail to learn the rules, you've lost the game before it has even begun.

Below is a summary of the three laws that will help you make the most of the power of belief.

#1. Law of choice.

This law states that *you can choose to believe anything you desire.* Practice replacing disempowering beliefs with empowering ones that support your goals.

#2. Law of cause and effect.

This law states that *what you believe affects your life.* Your thoughts dictate your actions and come with real consequences. To change your life, change your beliefs.

#3 Law of repetition.

This law states that *you can dramatically increase the intensity and power of your thoughts through repetition.* Repeat a thought in your head until it affects how you feel and what you do.

To sum up, because what you believe affects your life, choose empowering beliefs that serve you. Then, keep repeating them until they affect how you feel, what you do, and, eventually, the results you obtain.

4. The three Meta-Beliefs that rule them all

Meta-Beliefs are fundamental beliefs that make all the other beliefs possible.

Once internalized deeply enough, the following three Meta-Beliefs will restructure your belief system and change everything for you:

- Everything is possible
- Everything is learnable
- Every problem is solvable

Make these three Meta-Beliefs your mantras. Using the power of repetition, retrain your brain so that you can approach each new situation with a more empowering mindset.

Whenever you face an issue, remind yourself that everything is possible, everything is learnable, and every problem is solvable. Then, look for possible ways to move forward with your most important goals or solve your issues.

5. The Power of Subjective Reality

To transform the outer world, you must transform your inner world. To use the power of subjective reality, behave as though the outside world was a direct reflection of your inner thoughts and feelings. To do so, complete the following exercise:

Step #1. Close your eyes and imagine the outside world is merely a projection of your inside world. See yourself as being responsible for the state of the entire world.

Step #2. Now, look at areas of your life in which you're not taking full responsibility. Then, complete the following prompt:

If I was responsible for the state of the entire world, this is what I would do differently:

_____

_____

_____

_____

_____

Step #3. Imagine that you're the only playable character in the world. Knowing the world is the perfect reflection of your inner thoughts, what are the most empowering beliefs you could adopt to help you achieve anything you desire?

The most empowering beliefs I could adopt:

_____

_____

_____

Part II. Applying Extreme Leverage

To impact the world at scale, you must be able to deliver extraordinary results. And extraordinary results require not just an extraordinary mindset, but also extraordinary leverage.

As a reminder, below are the eight forms of leverage:

1. **Thoughts (size and intensity).** By thinking bigger, you act from a completely different place and magnify your impact. And by intensifying your thoughts, you make them more powerful.
2. **Thinking.** Accurate thinking makes each of your decisions far more impactful.
3. **Personal growth.** Working on yourself enables you to increase your impact dramatically.
4. **Technologies.** Technology is human labor on steroids. It enables you to multiply time and gather far more energy than you otherwise could.
5. **Focus.** A sustained focus over the long term activates the power of compounding that generates an extraordinary return on the time you have invested.
6. **Other people's time/energy.** Your time/energy is limited. Buying other people's time/energy is essential to generating more leverage.
7. **Money.** Money (yours or other people's money) is nothing more than stored time and energy. The more money you have, the more time and energy you can use to advance your vision.
8. **Knowledge.** Knowledge is the sum of the progress made by human civilization up until now. It's people's time and energy stored and curated over centuries for its usefulness.

On a scale from 1 to 10 (1 being poor, 10 being excellent), rate yourself on your current ability to use each form of leverage to achieve extraordinary results.

1. Thoughts (i.e. the size and intensity of your thoughts)

0 _____ 10

2. Thinking (i.e. the accuracy of your thinking)

0 _____ 10

3. Personal growth (i.e your level of self-mastery)

0 _____ 10

4. Technologies (i.e how effectively you use technology)

0 _____ 10

5. Focus (i.e. your long-term focus and level of consistency)

0 _____ 10

6. Other people's time/energy (i.e. how well you delegate and lead teams)

0 _____ 10

7. Money (i.e. your ability to make money and/or raise funds)

0 _____ 10

8. Knowledge (i.e. how well you learn and implement existing knowledge)

0 _____ 10

Now, what are the top 3 forms of leverage that if you were to focus on would allow you to scale your impact the most?

1.

2.

3.

Leverage #1—Thoughts (size and intensity)

Having bigger thoughts enables us to take impactful actions that will create extraordinary results.

Leverage #1a—Thoughts (size)

To disrupt yourself you must think bigger. Here are a few things you can do to think bigger:

- Surround yourself with people who set high standards for themselves
- Consume content from extraordinary people who you want to be like
- Find role models who inspire you in various areas of life
- Think bigger, more empowering thoughts, and write statements that you want to be true about yourself on a daily basis.

1) Destroying myths around thinking big

Failing to think big is one of the main reasons we grow slowly. It happens for the reasons below:

1. We were never taught we *could* think big. Nobody ever told us that we can think bigger and raise our standards. Therefore, like most people, we've learned to accept our "fate" and settled for mediocrity.

2. We were never taught *how* to think big. Neither our parents nor our teachers taught us how to use our mind to turn the invisible into the visible.

3. We believe extraordinary is not for us. We see ourselves as being normal, ordinary. And ordinary people cannot become extraordinary. We simply fail to understand that our future self could be a widely different and better person.

2) How to increase the size of your thinking

Thinking bigger is a learnable skill. To increase the size of your thinking, complete the following exercise:

Step #1. Let go of limitations. Think of the biggest vision possible. Focus on what you desire for yourself, your family, and the world as a whole. Remember, the stronger your desire, the better.

Step #2. 10X your vision. Make your vision even bigger. What would it look like if you multiply it by ten? Experiment with a level of thinking you've never experienced before. See how it makes you feel.

Step #3. Further expand your vision. Now, what would it look like if you multiplied it by one hundred? Notice how you feel. Do you feel uncomfortable? Insecure? Overwhelmed? Anxious? Or do you feel excited, empowered and alive?

Step #4. Ask yourself what if? Now, assume your vision is possible. Let your mind wander into the impossible future you desire. Notice any self-doubt that arises. Practice letting go of your limitations. Spend five minutes thinking of "what if."

Step #5. Remind yourself that if someone else can do it, you can too. Let go of the idea that others are smarter than you. Eliminate the belief that you can't learn what you need to learn to reach your goals.

Step #6. Repeat the process as often as necessary. Whenever possible, spend time alone thinking bigger thoughts. You can do so when taking a shower or going for a walk, or when you wake up or before you go to sleep. Thinking big is a skill. Practice it—often.

Additionally, I encourage you to write down your vision and update it on a regular basis.

3) "Impossible" is a point of view

Big thoughts that seem unrealistic today might not be tomorrow. Don't limit yourself to what you think is plausible. Instead, remind yourself that everything is possible. Reread the section on Meta-

Beliefs and keep the mantra "everything is possible" in the back of your mind.

4) Feeling good vs. doing good

Wanting to feel good without having to do anything is another form of instant gratification. To impact the world at scale, you must eradicate feel-good activities and destroy any sense of moral superiority. Instead, you must judge yourself on the size and impact of your actions.

Consider the following questions:

Are my thoughts and actions match my words? If I keep doing what I'm doing right now, am I likely to achieve the goals that I say I care about?

5) Purifying your thoughts

The quality of your thoughts will determine the quality of your life. To become extraordinary, let go of impure and disempowering thoughts and replace them with pure and empowering ones. To do this you must:

A. Let go of excellent and choose extraordinary. Continuously recommit to your vision and protect it from any internal attack (a negative mindset) or external attack (other people's thinking).

B. Avoid the pull toward mediocrity. By definition, most humans are average. That's why you must proactively design an empowering environment that will help you raise your standard and maintain it.

C. Accept that nobody can see what you see. Many people won't believe in you. Don't downgrade your vision thought. Instead, upgrade your thinking to match your vision.

D. Eliminate the negative voices inside your head. As you move toward becoming extraordinary, you must let go of the limitations imposed by your parents, teachers, or society.

Leverage #1b—Thoughts (intensity)

1. The size of your thoughts

Big thoughts have more power but require far more time and effort before they can impact the world.

2. Energizing your thoughts

You must energize your thoughts to give them power and allow them to generate tangible results in the real world. It entails the following:

1. Understanding the power of thoughts.
2. Strengthening your thoughts through repetition.
3. Marinating in your thoughts.
4. Infusing your thoughts with intense desire.

Step #1—Understanding the power of thoughts

Start leveraging the power of your thoughts by understanding the process through which thoughts become things:

- First, you have a thought.
- Second, you give that thought your attention.
- Third, that thought takes shape.

Reread the corresponding passage in the book as needed.

Step #2—Strengthening thoughts through repetition

For a thought to shape your reality, you must repeat it over and over. To do so:

1. Consume positive content daily
2. Write down affirmations
3. Think of your core beliefs during the day

Now, complete the following exercises :

What habit(s) could you put in place to ensure that you consume positive content every day? Write down your answer(s) below:

What (your habit(s)):

_____

_____

_____

When (your trigger(s)):

_____

_____

_____

For how long:

_____

_____

_____

Now, write down 3 affirmations that you'll repeat each day (You can use the 3 meta-beliefs or create your own affirmations.):

1.

2.

3.

Think of your core beliefs during the day whenever possible (For instance, whenever you're walking).

Step #3—Marinating in your thoughts

A thought gains power when you give it your attention. "Marinate" in your thoughts by doing the following exercises:

1. Embracing alone time.

Block out at least 15 minutes this week to spend time to think of one of your goals. Focus on the following things:

- **Clarify your vision.** Think of what you really want. Focus on what excites you. Write down ideas and refine them. Get more specific.
- **Look for opportunities.** Ask "how," "who," and "what" questions. How can I reach that goal? Who can help me? What would it take to make it happen? Tell your subconscious to come up with ideas and solutions. Let it help you and do some of the work in the background.
- **Strengthen your conviction.** Let your vision consume you. Allow yourself to believe it's possible. See yourself there. Build a strong sense of conviction.

2. Overcoming self-doubt

Experiencing self-doubt is normal. Allow negative feelings to be there and avoid beating yourself up. Meanwhile, keep focusing on the thoughts that will help you design the life you desire.

Notice when feelings of self-doubt arise. Observe the content of your thoughts. Then, reread part of the book and/or refocus on your vision.

3. Having faith in your vision

Identify a specific time during your day/week when you can marinate in your vision (i.e. commute to work, daily walk, shower, etc.).

Write down when you could focus on your vision during the week:

I will marinate in my vision when:

_____

_____

_____

4. Accepting loneliness

Remind yourself that you cannot be extraordinary by doing ordinary things.

Use your alone time to refine your vision, to protect it, and to strengthen your conviction.

Step #4—Strengthening your thoughts through desire

The major obstacle between you and your vision is a lack of desire. Desire gives intensity to your thoughts and drives you to keep moving despite the inevitable setbacks. That's why you must cultivate more of it.

The 3-step method to cultivate desire

Step #1—Uncover your desires through authenticity (Identify)

A. Fully embrace your ambitions

Try to write down in one or a few sentences what you want out of life. What do you secretly desire? Complete the writing prompt below:

If I were to fully embrace my ambitions I would:

_____

_____

_____

_____

_____

B. Gain clarity regarding who you want to become

As the business philosopher, Jim Rohn, said:

"Success is not to be pursued; it is to be attracted by the person you become."

Now, complete the prompt below.

To move closer to my vision, I need to become:

_____

_____

_____

_____

C. Identify the whys behind your goals

To stay motivated, use the following types of motivators:

- Ego: our desire to enhance our sense of self through external validation.
- Love: a sincere desire to contribute to the world.
- Fear: a desire to move away from what we don't like.
- Desire: Our innate desire to do and become more.

Write down what you could do to use each type of motivator.

I will use ego to motivate me by:

_____

_____

_____

I will use love to motivate me by:

_____

_____

_____

I will use fear to motivate me by:

_____

_____

I will use desire to motivate me by:

_____

_____

_____

Step #2—Strengthen your desire through specificity (Build)

Stack your whys

Using the table below, list all the reasons you have to reach your goals. Then, in the right column, write down which motivator(s) you can rely on to increase your desire (ego (E), love (L), fear (F), or desire (D)).

Reasons	Motivators (E, L, F, D)

Finally, go through your list and stack all your whys in your mind. Amplify them. Combine them. Practice strengthening your desire to move toward your vision.

Step #3—Maintain your desire through practice (Maintain)

To maintain desire over the long term, you can do the following:

A. Find inspiring models,

B. Consume inspirational content daily,

C. Take daily actions, and

D. Remind yourself of your whys on a consistent basis.

A. Find inspiring models

What someone else can do, you most likely can too. This is why, nothing is more inspiring than seeing another person doing extraordinary things.

Whenever you encounter someone you consider to be a role model for you, write down his or her name in the table below:

Name of the role model	Area of expertise

B. Consume inspirational content daily

When you stop moving toward your goals, you lose momentum. This is why you must cultivate desire daily.

Write down at least one thing that you can do each day to stay motivated (Read inspirational books, practice gratitude, etc.)

What I could do to stay motivated each day:

_____

_____

_____

C. Take daily actions

What you do every single day compounds over time and creates outstanding results.

Write down a couple of daily actions that would help you build momentum and make progress toward some of your current goals.

To move toward my goals, each day I could:

_____

_____

_____

D. Remind yourself of your whys on a consistent basis

Desire is a habit. You either cultivate it each day and strengthen its intensity, or you let it wither away, and you lose momentum.

Remind yourself of your whys on a regular basis. A good idea is to do so when you think of your vision (as you go to work, when walking, or when taking a shower).

Leverage #2—Thinking

By thinking more accurately, you can create effective strategies that, in turn, will help you take impactful actions.

I. The power of accurate thinking

1) Improving your model of reality

The closest your model of reality is to actual reality, the more you can impact the world. This is because, every decision you make places it on top of a solid foundation (i.e., an accurate model of reality). In short, you're interacting with the world as it *is* rather than *as you wish it to be.*

Now, complete the following prompt.

To improve my current model of reality I could:

_____

_____

_____

_____

2) strategy vs. tactics

Tactics can never create extraordinary results unless they are part of a well-thought-out strategy. As a reminder:

- A strategy is a plan of action you use to reach a specific goal.
- A tactic is a specific action or method that belongs to a larger strategy.

Think of a major goal you'd like to achieve.

My major goal:

_____

Now, try to articulate your strategy to reach that goal:

_____

_____

_____

_____

2. Overcome thinking biases

Rate yourself on a scale from 1 to 10 (1 being often, 10 being never) for each of the following thinking biases. In other words, how often you fall for them.

Sunk cost fallacy.

0 _____ 10

Correlation and causation.

0 _____ 10

Emotional reasoning.

0 _____ 10

Mistaking who you are today for who you will be tomorrow.

0 _____ 10

Believing bigger is harder.

0 _____ 10

Failing to understand exponential growth.

0 _____ 10

Leverage #3—Personal growth

Personal development is the ultimate leverage because it enables us to uncover our exceptional abilities and do the things that we once thought impossible

Rate your level of self-confidence, self-discipline, and grit on a scale from 1 to 10.

Self-confidence

0 _____ 10

Self-discipline

0 _____ 10

Grit

0 _____ 10

Strengthening self-confidence

To build more self-confidence, practice the following:

Repeat Meta-Beliefs and other empowering beliefs daily. When taking a shower, walking, or before going to bed, think of empowering beliefs that will help you build the life you desire.

Act accordingly. Positive self-talk must be backed up with concrete action. The more you act in line with your beliefs, the more you'll strengthen these beliefs.

Do what you're afraid of. Challenge yourself. Face your fears. As you move toward discomfort, you'll build more confidence over time.

Now, write down one specific thing you could do to help you strengthen your self-confidence

To strengthen my self-confidence I will:

_____

Building discipline

To build more self-discipline practice:

- Keeping promises to yourself, and
- Keeping promises to others.

To do so:

- Set small tasks each day and complete them
- Make fewer promises
- Set bigger goals over time

Now, write down below one specific thing that you could do to help you boost self-discipline for time.

To increase self-discipline I will:

_____

Cultivating extraordinary grit

Grit is often what separates ordinary people from extraordinary ones. Below are a few things you can do to develop more grit and determination:

A. Expect failures and prepare for the worst

B. Understand that when you feel like giving up it means the game is on.

C. Build the identity of someone who never quits

D. See failure as a test from the universe

E. Focus on the process

F. Reframe failure

Think of a major life goal you'd like to achieve. Write it down below.

My major goal:

_____

Now, imagine the absolute worst-case scenario and write it down below.

_____

_____

_____

Spend a moment to envision yourself going through it. Then, see yourself moving forward, nevertheless, with even more motivation than before.

Remind yourself that you're not the type of person who quits. Write down below what you would say to yourself when you feel like giving up (ex: I never quit. That's not who I am.)

_____

_____

_____

Leverage #4—Technology

Technology enables you to gather more energy by using new tools that can replace human labor or do things that no human can do.

1. How to use technology to scale your impact

1) Automation and processes

How can you use automation and processes in order to multiply your impact? Write down below three specific things you could do.

1.

2.

3.

2) Algorithms

What specific algorithms could you use in order to further magnify your impact long term?

Write down your answers below.

_____

_____

_____

Leverage #5—Focus

Focus is the ability to gather our energy and direct it toward a specific goal for long enough to make it a reality.

There are roughly three types of focus:

- Short-term focus (concentration),
- Transitional focus (planning/routine), and
- Long-term focus (vision).

What can you do to increase short-term, transitional, and long-term focus?

Complete the exercise below.

To improve my short-term focus (concentration), I will eliminate internal and external distractions by:

_____

_____

_____

To improve my transitional focus (planning/routine), I will:

_____

_____

_____

To improve your long-term focus, you need to refine your vision. To help you do so, complete the exercises below.

Think of your ideal future

Use the space below to write down any ideas or visions you have regarding your ideal future. What do you want to do? What kind of person do you want to become? If you could accomplish the extraordinary, what would make you feel most proud? Let go of any fear or limitations. Forget about being realistic.

My ideal future:

_____

_____

_____

Identify the gaps

To move closer to your vision, you will need to fill in the gaps in terms of:

- Skills,
- Character traits,
- Network, and
- Resources/people.

Answer the following questions.

What specific skills do I need to learn?

_____

_____

_____

_____

_____

What character traits do I need to develop?

_____

_____

_____

_____

_____

Who do I need to surround myself with?

_____

_____

_____

_____

Leverage #6—Other people's time/energy

Leveraging other people's time and energy entails working with freelancers, contractors, and/or building teams to increase the amount of energy available to move you closer to your vision.

As you work on scaling your venture and magnify your impact, consider the following steps:

1. Test
2. Amplify what works
3. Amplify even more
4. Create processes
5. Build teams/find top talent
6. Remove yourself

Now, select one project that you're currently working on. Then, think of how well you fare for each step above. What could you change or improve on? Should you test more, amplify what works, refine your processes, build a team, or work on removing yourself?

Leverage #7—Money

Money is simply a tool that enables you to scale your impact.

Roughly speaking, there are two different ways to use money to amplify your impact:

1. Investing in yourself
2. Investing in your business

1. Investing in yourself

Answer the following questions.

Find where you're lacking the skills needed to scale your impact. What's your limiting factor? Where are you lacking the skills needed to scale your impact?

My limiting factor is:

_____

_____

_____

What could you do specifically to acquire those skills in the near future?

My plan to acquire those skills:

_____

_____

_____

_____

_____

2. Invest in your business

If you have a business or a venture you're currently working on, what could you do specifically to invest in it so as to scale and multiply your impact? (i.e. invest in marketing, work with coaches, buy courses, join masterminds, etc.)?

Write down your answers below.

_____

_____

_____

_____

_____

How to accumulate money

In addition to making money yourself, there are other ways that you can gather more money in order to scale your impact. If you need to borrow or raise money, what could you do specifically to help you do so? (contacting a friend, reading books, joining relevant groups online, etc.)?

Brainstorm ideas using the space below.

_____

_____

_____

_____

_____

Increasing the velocity of money

Money sitting in a bank isn't that useful. How could you put your money to work so as to accelerate your personal growth and/or your business?

Write down things you could do to increase the velocity of your money.

_____

_____

_____

_____

Leverage #8—Knowledge

Leveraging knowledge means leveraging the collective time of the entire world population (past and present).

Remember, when we learn, we usually go through the three stages below:

1. **Knowing.** It's when you know something intellectually.

2. **Doing.** It's when you actually *do* something with the information you consume.

3. **Living.** It's when you do something consistently until you turn intellectual knowledge into practical skills.

Develop a mastery mindset

Assess your level of mastery by rating yourself on a scale from 1 to 10 for the following statement (1 being false, 0 being true).

I'm a master of the process. I'm consistent.

0 _____ 10

I'm a master of implementation. I get things done.

0 _____ 10

I'm a master of humility. I seek to learn rather than being right.

0 _____ 10

I'm a master of repetition. I practice daily skills that matter to me.

0 _____ 10

I'm a master of grit. I don't stop until I achieve my goals.

0 _____ 10

I'm a master of faith. I trust the process and keep believing.

0 _____ 10

I'm a master of long-term thinking.

0 _____ 10

Invert your learning/action ratio

To acquire invaluable skills and much needed experience, you need to take more action and spend less time "learning." Answer the following questions.

In what ways are you learning too much, consuming more information than you need to?

_____

_____

_____

Now, what could you do specifically to take more action?

_____

_____

_____

Acquiring meta-skills

What meta-skills do you need to acquire in priority in order to scale your impact and make a bigger difference with your work?

Write them down below.

_____

_____

_____

_____

_____

MASTER YOUR EMOTIONS
(PREVIEW)

66 The mind is its own place, and in itself can make a heaven of Hell, a hell of Heaven.

— JOHN MILTON, POET.

We all experience a wide range of emotions throughout our lives. I had to admit, while writing this book, I experienced highs and lows myself. At first, I was filled with excitement and thrilled at the idea of providing people with a guide to help them understand their emotions. I imagined how readers' lives would improve as they learned to control their emotions. My motivation was high and I couldn't help but imagine how great the book would be.

Or so I thought.

After the initial excitement, the time came to sit down to write the actual book, and that's when the excitement wore off pretty quickly. Suddenly ideas that looked great in my mind felt dull. My writing seemed boring, and I felt as though I had nothing substantive or valuable to contribute.

Sitting at my desk and writing became more challenging each day. I started losing confidence. Who was I to write a book about emotions if I couldn't even master my own emotions? How ironic! I considered giving up. There are already plenty of books on the topic, so why add one more?

At the same time, I realized this book was a perfect opportunity to work on my emotional issues. And who doesn't suffer from negative emotions from time to time? We all have highs and lows, don't we? The key is what we *do* with our lows. Are we using our emotions to grow and learn or are we beating ourselves up over them?

So, let's talk about *your* emotions now. Let me start by asking you this:

How do you feel right now?

Knowing how you feel is the first step toward taking control of your emotions. You may have spent so much time internalizing you've lost touch with your feelings. Perhaps you answered as follows: "I feel this book could be useful," or "I really feel I could learn something from this book."

However, none of these answers reflect on how you feel. You don't 'feel like this,' or 'feel like that,' you simply 'feel.' You don't 'feel like' this book could be useful, you 'think' this book could be useful, and that generates an emotion which makes you 'feel' excited about reading it. Feelings manifest as physical sensations in your body, not as an idea in your mind. Perhaps, the reason the word 'feel' is so often overused or misused is because we don't want to talk about our emotions.

So, how do you feel now?

Why is it important to talk about emotions?

How you feel determines the quality of your life. Your emotions can make your life miserable or truly magical. That's why they are among the most essential things on which to focus. Your emotions color all your experiences. When you feel good, everything seems, feels, or tastes better. You also think better thoughts. Your energy levels are higher and possibilities seem limitless. Conversely, when you feel depressed, everything seems dull. You have little energy and you become unmotivated. You feel stuck in a place (mentally and physically) you don't want to be, and the future looks gloomy.

Your emotions can also act as a powerful guide. They can tell you something is wrong and allow you to make changes in your life. As such, they may be among the most powerful personal growth tools you have.

Sadly, neither your teachers nor your parents taught you how emotions work or how to control them. I find it ironic that just about anything comes with a how-to manual, while your mind doesn't. You've never received an instruction manual to teach you how your mind works and how to use it to better manage your emotions, have you? I haven't. In fact, until now, I doubt one even existed.

What you'll learn in this book

This book is the how-to manual your parents should have given you at birth. It's the instruction manual you should have received at school. In it, I'll share everything you need to know about emotions so you can overcome your fears and limitations and become the type of person you want to be.

More specifically, this book will help you:

- Understand what emotions are and how they impact your life
- Understand how emotions form and how you can use them for your personal growth
- Identify negative emotions that control your life and learn to overcome them
- Change your story to take better control over your life and create a more compelling future,
- Reprogram your mind to experience more positive emotions.
- Deal with negative emotions and condition your mind to create more positive ones

- Gain all the tools you need to start recognizing and controlling your emotions

Here is a more detailed summary of what you'll learn in this book:

In **Part I**, we'll discuss what emotions are. You'll learn why your brain is wired to focus on negativity and what you can do to counter this effect. You'll also discover how your beliefs impinge upon your emotions. Finally, you'll learn how negative emotions work and why they are so tricky.

In **Part II**, we'll go over the things that directly impact your emotions. You'll understand the roles your body, your thoughts, your words, or your sleep, play in your life and how you can use them to change your emotions.

In **Part III**, you'll learn how emotions form and how to condition your mind to experience more positive emotions.

And finally, in **Part IV**, we'll discuss how to use your emotions as a tool for personal growth. You'll learn why you experience emotions such as fear or depression and how they work.

Let's get started.

To start mastering your emotions today go to

mybook.to/Master_Emotions

I. What emotions are

Have you ever wondered what emotions are and what purpose they serve?

In this section, we'll discuss how your survival mechanism affects your emotions. Then, we'll explain what the 'ego' is and how it impacts your emotions. Finally, we'll discover the mechanism behind emotions and learn why it can be so hard to deal with negative ones.

Why people have a bias towards negativity

Your brain is designed for survival, which explains why you're able to read this book at this very moment. When you think about it, the probability of you being born was extremely low. For this miracle to happen, all the generations before you had to survive long enough to procreate. In their quest for survival and procreation, they must have faced death hundreds or perhaps thousands of times.

Fortunately, unlike your ancestors, you're (probably) not facing death every day. In fact, in many parts of the world, life has never been safer. Yet, your survival mechanism hasn't changed much. Your brain still scans your environment looking for potential threats.

In many ways, some parts of your brain have become obsolete. While you may not be seconds away from being eaten by a predator, your brain still gives significantly more weight to adverse events than to positive ones.

Fear of rejection is one example of a bias toward negativity. In the past, being rejected by your tribe would reduce your chances of survival significantly. Therefore, you learned to look for any sign of rejection, and this became hardwired in your brain.

Nowadays, being rejected often carries little or no consequence to your long-term survival. You can be hated by the entire world and still have a job, a roof and plenty of food on the table, yet, your brain remains programmed to perceive rejection as a threat to your survival.

This hardwiring is why rejection can be so painful. While you know most rejections are no big deal, you nevertheless feel the emotional pain. If you listen to your mind, you may even create a whole drama around it. You may believe you aren't worthy of love and dwell on a rejection for days or weeks. Worse still, you may become depressed as a result of this rejection.

One single criticism can often outweigh hundreds of positive ones. That's why, an author with fifty 5-star reviews, is likely to feel terrible when they receive a single 1-star review. While the author understands the 1-star review isn't a threat to her survival, her authorial brain doesn't. It likely interprets the negative review as a threat to her ego which triggers an emotional reaction.

The fear of rejection can also lead you to over-dramatize events. If your boss criticized you at work, your brain might see the criticism as a threat and you now think, "What if my boss fires me? What if I can't find a job quickly enough and my wife leaves me? What about my kids? What if I can't see them again?"

While you are fortunate to have such a useful survival mechanism, it is also your responsibility to separate real threats from imaginary ones. If you don't, you'll experience unnecessary pain and worry that will negatively impact the quality of your life. To overcome this bias towards negativity, you must reprogram your mind. One of a human being's greatest powers is our ability to use our thoughts to shape our reality and interpret events in a more empowering way. This book will teach you how to do this.

Why your brain's job isn't to make you happy

Your brain's primary responsibility is not to make you happy, but to ensure your survival. Thus, if you want to be happy, you must actively take control of your emotions rather than hoping you'll be happy because it's your natural state. In the following section, we'll discuss what happiness is and how it works.

How dopamine can mess with your happiness

Dopamine is a neurotransmitter that, among other functions, plays a significant role in rewarding certain behaviors. When dopamine releases into specific areas of your brain—the pleasure centers—you get an intense sense of wellbeing similar to a high. This sense of wellbeing is what happens during exercise, when you gamble, have sex, or eat great food.

One of the roles of dopamine is to ensure you look for food so you don't die of starvation, and you search for a mate so you can reproduce. Without dopamine, our species would likely be extinct by now. It's a pretty good thing, right?

Well, yes and no. In today's world, this reward system is, in many cases, obsolete. In the past, dopamine directly linked to our survival, now, it can be stimulated artificially. A great example of this effect is social media, which uses psychology to suck as much time as possible out of your life. Have you noticed all these notifications that pop up regularly? They're used to trigger a release of dopamine so you stay connected, and the longer you stay connected, the more money the services make. Watching pornography or gambling also leads to a release of dopamine which can make these activities highly addictive.

Fortunately, we don't need to act each time our brain releases dopamine. For instance, we don't need to continuously check our Facebook newsfeeds just because it gives us a pleasurable shot of dopamine.

Today's society is selling a version of happiness that can make us *un*happy. We've become addicted to dopamine mainly because of marketers who have found effective ways to exploit our brains. We receive multiple shots of dopamine throughout the day and we love it. But is that the same thing as happiness?

Worse than that, dopamine can create real addictions with severe consequences on our health. Research conducted at Tulane University showed that, when permitted to self-stimulate their pleasure center, participants did it an average of forty times per minute. They chose the stimulation of their pleasure center over food, even refusing to eat when hungry!

Korean, Lee Seung Seop is an extreme case of this syndrome. In 2005, Mr Seop died after playing a video game for fifty-eight hours straight with very little food or water, and no sleep. The subsequent investigation concluded the cause of death was heart failure induced by exhaustion and dehydration. He was only twenty-eight years old.

To take control of your emotions, you must understand the role dopamine plays and how it affects your happiness. Are you addicted to your phone? Are you glued to your TV? Or maybe you spend too much time playing video games. Most of us are addicted to something. For some people it's obvious, but for others, it's more subtle. For instance, you could be addicted to thinking. To better control your emotions, you must recognize and shed the light on your addictions as they can rob you of your happiness.

The 'one day I will' myth

Do you believe that one day you will achieve your dream and finally be happy? It is unlikely to happen. You may (and I hope you will) achieve your goal, but you won't live 'happily ever after.' This thinking is just another trick your mind plays on you.

Your mind quickly acclimates to new situations, which is probably the result of evolution and our need to adapt continually to survive and reproduce. This acclimatization is also probably why the new car or house you want will only make you happy for a while. Once the initial excitement wears off, you'll move on to crave the next exciting thing. This phenomenon is known as 'hedonic adaptation.'

How hedonic adaptation works

Let me share an interesting study that will likely change the way you see happiness. This study, which was conducted in 1978 on lottery winners and paraplegics, was incredibly eye-opening for me. The investigation evaluated how winning the lottery or becoming a paraplegic influence happiness:

The study found that one year after the event, both groups were just as happy as they were beforehand. Yes, just as happy (or unhappy). You can find more about it by watching Dan Gilbert's TED Talk, The Surprising Science of Happiness.

Perhaps you believe that you'll be happy once you've 'made it.' But, as the above study on happiness shows, this is simply not true. No matter what happens to you, your mind works by reverting to your predetermined level of happiness once you've adapted to the new event.

Does that mean you can't be happier than you are right now? No. What it means is that, in the long run, external events have minimal impact on your level of happiness.

In fact, according to Sonja Lyubomirsky, author of *The How of Happiness*, fifty percent of our happiness is determined by genetics, forty percent by internal factors, and only ten percent by external factors. These external factors include such things as whether we're single or married, rich or poor, and similar social influences.

The influence of external factors is probably way less than you thought. The bottom line is this: Your attitude towards life influences your happiness, not what happens to you.

By now, you understand how your survival mechanism negatively impacts your emotions and prevents you from experiencing more joy and happiness in your life. In the next section, we'll learn about the ego.

To read more visit my author page at:

amazon.com/author/thibautmeurisse

OTHER BOOKS BY THE AUTHORS:

Mastery Series

1. Master Your Emotions: A Practical Guide to Overcome Negativity and Better Manage Your Feelings

2. Master Your Motivation: A Practical Guide to Unstick Yourself, Build Momentum and Sustain Long-Term Motivation

3. Master Your Focus: A Practical Guide to Stop Chasing the Next Thing and Focus on What Matters Until It's Done

4. Master Your Destiny: A Practical Guide to Rewrite Your Story and Become the Person You Want to Be

5. Master Your Thinking: A Practical Guide to Align Yourself with Reality and Achieve Tangible Results in the Real World

6. Master Your Success: Timeless Principles to Develop Inner Confidence and Create Authentic Success

7. Master Your Beliefs: A Practical Guide to Stop Doubting Yourself and Build Unshakeable Confidence

8. Master Your Time: A Practical Guide to Increase Your Productivity and Use Your Time Meaningfully

9. Master Your Learning: A Practical Guide to Learn More Deeply, Retain Information Longer and Become a Lifelong Learner

Productivity Series

Other books

Think Better Thoughts: 100 Limiting Beliefs that Hinder Your Potential (and How to Eliminate Them)

Upgrade Yourself: Simple Strategies to Transform Your Mindset, Improve Your Habits and Change Your Life

Success is Inevitable: 17 Laws to Unlock Your Hidden Potential, Skyrocket Your Confidence and Get What You Want From Life

Wake Up Call: How To Take Control Of Your Morning And Transform Your Life

ABOUT THE AUTHOR

THIBAUT MEURISSE

Thibaut is the author of over 20 books including the #1 Amazon Bestseller, "Master Your Emotions" which has sold over 300,000 copies and has been translated into more than 20 languages including French, Spanish, German, Chinese, Thai, and Portuguese.

Thibaut's mission is to help ordinary people attain extraordinary results.

If you like simple practical and inspiring books, and are committed to improve your life, you'll love his work.

amazon.com/author/thibautmeurisse
thibautmeurisse.com
thibaut.meurisse@gmail.com

Made in United States
Troutdale, OR
03/17/2024